D0116231

The Transcontinental Railroad and Westward Expansion

Chasing the American Frontier

The Transcontinental Railroad and Westward Expansion

Chasing the American Frontier

Tim McNeese

Enslow Publishers, Inc.
40 Industrial Road
Box 398
Berkeley Heights, NJ 07922
USA
        http://www.enslow.com

Library of Congress Cataloging-in-Publication Data

McNeese, Tim.
    The Transcontinental Railroad and westward expansion : chasing the
American frontier / Tim McNeese.
      p. cm. — (The American saga)
    Includes bibliographical references and index.
    ISBN 0-7660-2572-1
    1. Pacific railroads—Juvenile literature. I. Title. II. Series.
TF25.P23M43 2006
385.0979—dc22

                            2005030209

Printed in the United States of America

10 9 8 7 6 5 4 3 2 1

To Our Readers:
We have done our best to make sure all Internet Addresses in this book were
active and appropriate when we went to press. However, the author and the
publisher have no control over and assume no liability for the material available
on those Internet sites or on other Web sites they may link to. Any comments or
suggestions can be sent by e-mail to comments@enslow.com or to the address on
the back cover.

Illustration Credits: ©Andre Jenny/The Image Works, p. 104; © Corel
Corporation, pp. 3 (center), 6, 27, 31, 40, 44, 106, 107; Denver Public
Library, Western History Collection, pp. 3 (left), 11, 15, 50, 63, 81, 112
(bottom); *Dictionary of American Portraits*, published by Dover
Publications, Inc., in 1967, pp. 9; *Engraving by H. B. Hall's Sons,
Dictionary of American Portraits*, published by Dover Publications, Inc.,
in 1967, pp. 74, 112 (top); Enslow Publishers, Inc., pp. 29, 96, 110 (top);
Library of Congress, pp. 3 (right), 18, 23, 33, 34, 36, 42, 48, 52, 53, 61, 64,
75, 77, 83, 86, 92, 95, 110 (bottom two photos), 111; North Wind Picture
Archives, p. 98; ©Roger-Viollet/Topham/The Image Works, pp. 105, 113.

Cover Illustration: © Corel Corporation (large photo); ©Roger-
Viollet/Topham/The Image Works (inset).

Contents

Work on the Central Pacific Railroad slowed once it reached the Sierra Nevada mountains.

"Without Them It Would Be Impossible"

By the spring of 1865, construction on the western end of the first railroad across America was coming to an end. During the previous thirty years, dozens of railroads had been built east of the Mississippi River. Each one helped move Americans farther west. There was great excitement across the country during the 1850s as plans developed to build a railroad from Nebraska to California. A gold rush during the late 1840s in California lured tens of thousands to the mining camps. By 1850, California became a state.

To bridge the wide-open spaces between Nebraska and California, a railroad was needed. The Central Pacific (CP) Railroad received the contracts to build the line from California east. At the same time, another railroad, the Union Pacific (UP), was to build from Omaha, Nebraska, to the west. Somewhere in the middle, the two railroads would join their rails together. Through 1864, the Central Pacific built its line quickly, making good time. Then, it reached a giant natural barrier—a mountain range called the Sierra Nevadas.

But the problem facing the Central Pacific that spring was not the mountains. It was a lack of workers. The railroad bosses needed at least ten thousand men to work on the rail line. But they had fewer than one thousand workers available. The problem was gold and silver. California was home to well over one hundred thousand people. But many would not work for the railroad. They thought they could make more money digging for gold. Then, silver strikes in neighboring Nevada lured thousands more to seek their fortune. Sometimes, the railroad hired such men to work. They transported them by rail to the work sites. The men might work a week, then they took off for the mining camps. They used the railroad to get a free ride to the silver diggings. By the spring of 1865, the Central Pacific had laid fewer than forty miles of track during the previous eighteen months.

Other labor problems plagued the Central Pacific. Workers began going out on strike, demanding higher pay. Frustrated Central Pacific officials did not know what to do. Mileage counted: The U.S. government paid the railroads for every mile of track they laid. Then, in desperation, one of the Central Pacific's directors, Charles Crocker, suggested a solution. He proposed to the CP superintendent of construction, James Harvey Strobridge, that he hire a different group of workers. "Hire some Chinese," Crocker ordered Strobridge.[1]

After all, California was home to tens of thousands of Chinese laborers. Many had come to California because of the gold rush. By the mid-1860s, there were at least sixty thousand young Chinese men in California.[2] Crocker reminded Strobridge of the number of available Chinese workers. He told him that dozens of Chinese men had recently helped build the Dutch Flat and Donner Lake Wagon Road.

Charles Crocker

While the suggestion made sense, Strobridge would not agree. A powerful man with a violent temper, Strobridge roared his disapproval: "I will not boss Chinese!"[3] Strobridge was like many white men in California in the 1860s. He did not appreciate the Chinese. These immigrants were often mistreated by whites. They had to live in their own communities and accept any jobs given them. Thousands worked as cooks, gardeners, laundrymen, and house servants. To many nineteenth-century Americans, their customs were strange. They ate seemingly peculiar foods, and they were not Christians. Strobridge told Crocker that white workers would not work with Chinese laborers. He said the Chinese were too small, too skinny to work as railroad builders. The average Chinese worker weighed less than 120 pounds and was shorter than four feet ten inches in height.[4] But Crocker insisted.

"They built the Great Wall of China, didn't they," Crocker told Strobridge. "Who said laborers have to be white to build railroads?"[5]

Reluctantly, Strobridge agreed. He hired a gang of fifty Chinese laborers. He would work them hard and see if they could keep up. It would be a test Strobridge knew the Chinese workers would fail.

That March, Strobridge put the Chinese laborers to work. They filled and hauled wheelbarrows filled with earth. They did not need any important skills. They just had to work hard. Many white railroad workers did not want to work next to these new Chinese workers. They were prejudiced against these foreign workmen. So, Strobridge put the Chinese laborers in their own gangs.

When the Chinese workers reached their first work site, white rail crews jeered at them. The white workers did not believe these foreign workmen could do hard railroad work. In fact, as the Chinese worked, they removed small shovelfuls of earth. They moved their wheelbarrows with less earth than the non-Chinese workers. But they worked almost nonstop. Unlike the other workers, they did not take many breaks. They only halted their work a few times a day to sip their favorite drink—hot tea. By the end of the first day, the Chinese had removed more dirt. They had built a smoother base for rails to be laid than the white crews had built.

The following morning, the non-Chinese crews did not intend to be shown up by these new Chinese workers

Members of a Union Pacific Railroad crew, some of them Chinese, take a break on a railroad handcar.

again. They worked faster, took fewer breaks, and cut their lunchtime in half. But, still, the Chinese workers kept up their pace. By the end of the first week, the Chinese work gangs had completed the longest length of base for laying track of any of the gangs along the line. Although Strobridge had at first refused to "boss"

Chinese workers, he soon sent word to his own bosses: He wanted more Chinese laborers.

Strobridge hired another fifty Chinese workers, then another fifty. Soon, hundreds of Chinese were at work on the Central Pacific's railroad. They were given all the difficult jobs. These included digging, cutting down trees, and cutting or using explosives to blast out tunnels through the granite walls of the Sierra Nevadas. Many of the Chinese workers feared Strobridge. He was loud and got angry easily. He had lost an eye in an explosion during some of the earlier construction and wore an eye patch. The Chinese laborers called him "One Eye Bossy Man."[6]

In a short time, the Central Pacific was hiring more Chinese workers through private companies. White workers were paid two dollars a day for their work, plus food and a place to sleep. Chinese workers might only receive between four dollars and eight dollars a month.[7] Some of the companies were Chinese owned. Many of these employment companies went to China and hired workers to come to America. The Chinese workers needed a special diet. The Central Pacific agreed to provide such foods as Chinese bacon, dried fish, oysters, pork, poultry, bamboo sprouts, sweet rice crackers, salted cabbage, rice and, of course, tea.

The Chinese proved themselves excellent workers. As the journalist Charles Nordhoff described them:

> They do not drink or fight or strike . . . and it is always said of them that they are very cleanly in their habits. It is the custom among them, after

they have had their suppers every evening, to bathe with the help of small tubs. I doubt if the white laborers do as much.[8]

Chinese laborers worked well together in gangs. Those who came from the same province in China worked with one another. They spoke the same regional dialect of the Chinese language. The Chinese workers were also sick less often than white workers. This was, perhaps, because they boiled their water before making their tea. Their diet of fish, bamboo shoots, and other vegetables was healthier than the average white worker's diet of beef and beans. The Chinese also bathed every day, a common custom in China. In contrast, the average nineteenth-century American might, at best, bathe once a week. These things kept the Chinese workers healthy.

By May 1865, the Central Pacific had organized hundreds of Chinese workers into work gangs. Each gang numbered between twelve and twenty men. That same month, one railroad official wrote a letter to a congressman: "I can assure you the Chinese are moving the earth and rock rapidly. They prove nearly equal to white men in the amount of labor they perform, and are far more reliable." He added: "without them it would be impossible to go on with the work."[9] Before June, the Central Pacific was employing more than seven thousand Chinese workers. By comparison, there were only two thousand white CP laborers. By year's end, one Central Pacific report stated: "The Chinese experiment has proved eminently successful."[10]

Blasting Through the Sierra Nevadas

The Chinese workers Strobridge first hired were used only as manual laborers. But CP officials soon realized the Chinese had specific skills. The railroad needed to pass through the rugged Sierra Nevadas. The Chinese had a knowledge of explosives. The mountain chain was a monumental barrier. Tens of thousands of tons of hard rock, especially granite, would need removing. Construction crews would have to drill fifteen tunnels. The longest would be a quarter mile long. Long, deep ravines would need filling. Many railroad bridges, called trestles, would have to be built of redwood and spruce logs.

The Chinese workers showed their true talent was with explosives. (Chinese scientists had discovered the formula for "gunpowder" in the seventh century A.D.) During the summer of 1865, the Central Pacific faced a rugged mountain of shale the workers called "Cape Horn." It rose above the American River to heights above two thousand feet. There were no trails along the cliff side. The workers needed to carve a shelf along the summit for a train to run along. To blast out a rock shelf, men would have to be lowered down the cliff side in baskets. Then, they would place the black powder charges, light the fuses, and yell to the men above to pull them up out of the way of the explosion.

As engineers faced "Cape Horn," they did not believe the work could be done.

Finally, a Chinese foreman approached Strobridge. He told the feared boss that he and his fellow workers could do the job. Strobridge agreed to let them try. He even agreed to the workers' requests for reeds to be delivered to the work site. The Chinese laborers wove special reed baskets. They were small and round, light and sturdy. Each held one man by a central cable. Over the next few years, the Chinese worked with explosives

This engraving, which appeared in the May 29, 1869 *Harper's Weekly*, shows European- and Asian-American workers as they blast through a rock formation.

and carved a rail line out of the stubborn mountain rock. How many Chinese workers were killed while working with black powder and another explosive material, nitroglycerin, is unknown. The Central Pacific did not keep track of the Chinese death toll. Overall, perhaps twelve hundred Chinese workers were killed working for the Central Pacific.[11] However, the Chinese worked from the summer of 1865 through the spring of 1866 on the mountain. They blasted a rock shelf, created a roadbed, and laid the track.

Perhaps the most difficult challenge the Chinese workers faced in the Sierra Nevadas was excavating the Summit Tunnel. It was the sixth tunnel built on the western side of the mountains. The tunnel measured nearly seventeen hundred feet in length. It was cut out at an elevation of seven thousand feet.[12] The tunnel stood twenty feet high.[13] Crocker put five hundred Chinese laborers to work on Summit Tunnel in the spring of 1866. At first, the blasting crews used black powder to remove the granite rock. But the rock was sometimes so hard it shot back out of the predrilled holes. Sometimes, excavation might only move ahead seven or eight inches a day. In just one day, blasting crews might use up to five hundred kegs of black powder. They might still make little progress along the mountain face.

A newspaper reporter saw the Central Pacific's Chinese workers trying to blast through the Sierra Nevadas near Donner Lake:

> Through the gathering shades of night, immense
> volumes of fire and dense clouds of smoke from

the mountainside, as if a mighty volcano was rending it to atoms. Huge masses of rocks and debris were rent and heaved up in the commotion; then ... came the thunders of explosion like a lightning stroke, reverberating along the hills and canyons, as if the whole artillery of Heaven was in play.[14]

The Chinese workers did not just blast tunnels. They also had to create a roadbed along the cliff faces. This was extremely dangerous. Chinese workers had to clear the shelf they were creating of all debris and rock, as well as trees. Some of these trees were hundreds of feet tall. One three-hundred-man Chinese gang spent ten workdays clearing the right-of-way for just one mile of track. Ten barrels of black powder might be used to remove just one tree. Each explosion sent rock and debris, as well as tree splinters, flying in every direction. Men were killed by these flying missiles.

By 1867, CP officials, including Crocker and Strobridge, began allowing the use of nitroglycerin as an explosive. The chemical explosive was fairly new and extremely dangerous. But it was eight times more powerful than black powder. It could blast away a greater amount of granite using a smaller drilled hole. Because it was so unstable, it was mixed on site.

Nitroglycerin increased progress at construction sites, such as Summit Tunnel, by 50 percent. As one railroad official wrote to another: "[Crocker] has just come from the tunnel and he thinks some of them are

Chinese workers are seen near what would become the first opening of the Summit Tunnel.

making three feet per day. Hurrah! For nitroglycerine."[15] But nitro killed more Chinese workers. After only a few months of use, Crocker ordered his workers to stop using it.

As deadly as the explosives work was, Chinese laborers suffered other dangers working in the mountains. For one, the weather could kill as easily as black powder or nitroglycerin. High in the mountains, snows fell regularly. In all, work crews faced forty-four snowstorms.[16]

The worst storm struck the Chinese laborers and other railroad workers in 1866. It began on the afternoon of February 18 and did not end until 10 p.m. four days later. Six feet of snow covered the work sites. It sometimes buried the workers. Chinese laborers tunneled beneath snowdrifts piled up sixty feet high.[17] Deadly avalanches took place. One railroad official recorded the results of one: "Snow slides carried away our camps and we lost a good many men in those slides . . . Many of them we did not find until the next season when the snow melted."[18]

Carving a rail path through the Sierra Nevadas was not completed until the fall of 1868. Workers had toiled for more than three years in the hard rock mountains. When the work was completed, the Chinese workers were recognized for all their hard work. As one newspaper reporter wrote, each Chinese worker "with his patient toil, directed by American energy and backed by American capital, has broken down the great barrier at last and opened over it the greatest highway yet created for the march of commerce and civilization around the globe."[19]

The following year, the first American transcontinental railroad was completed. The two railroads—the Central Pacific and the Union Pacific—joined rails at Promontory Point, Utah, in May 1869. That year, the United States of America was just short of a century old. From the 1770s until 1869, Americans pushed across a continent. They settled new lands where American Indians had lived for thousands of years. But the Transcontinental Railroad did not mark the end of the American frontier. It signaled the nation was linked from the Atlantic to the Pacific, "from sea to shining sea."

Between the Known and the Unknown

For thousands of years, people have lived in the Americas. These lands include modern-day North and South America, as well as Central America and the Caribbean Islands. American Indian groups established their villages and towns. Each tribe created its own culture and ways of life. When Columbus arrived in 1492, North America (present-day United States, Canada, and Mexico) was home to millions of native residents. With the arrival of Europeans like Columbus, the history of all the Americas was going to change.

Soon, other European explorers reached the Western Hemisphere, a term referring to all the Americas. While Columbus, an Italian, sailed in the name of the king and queen of Spain, others arrived in the Americas sponsored by the monarchs of Portugal, France, England, Holland, and other European countries. During the century following Columbus's arrival, Europeans came over by the thousands. They were settlers, priests, soldiers, farmers, and others who established outposts, forts, and trading colonies.

They established thirteen English colonies up and down the Atlantic seaboard. Many of those who settled in those colonies were of English descent. But others came from France, Holland, Germany, Sweden, Ireland, Scotland, and dozens of other places. Africans were also brought to America by force during the early seventeenth century. They had been enslaved and were forced to work on farms and in white people's homes. By 1750, all thirteen of these colonies were well established. Some were home to important colonial cities, such as Boston, New York, Philadelphia, and Charleston, South Carolina. In most places, American Indians were forced to surrender their traditional lands.

The British Colonial Frontier

For more than 150 years, the people in the British colonies clung to their settlements, towns, and cities along the coast. They rarely moved more than one hundred miles inland from the ocean. The threat of American Indians to the west kept them from moving farther west. These Indians wanted to stop the advance of European colonists. European colonization meant the loss of Indian lands. But after 1750, a great movement of colonists began taking place. Many of these colonists thought of themselves as "Americans." Their experiences made up the first of the American frontiers. They built their cabins and houses in the wilderness. They were many different types of people. Some were gentlemen in Jamestown looking for gold.

The Pilgrims did not travel too far from where they landed during the first years of their settlement. Most of the time, they used American Indian trails or blazed ones of their own.

Others were pious Pilgrims in Plymouth. Still others were German Jews from Salzburg who settled in North Carolina. These early immigrants became settlers who experienced difficult times. Some faced disease, starvation, or American Indian attack. Sometimes they were attacked by other Europeans. Many died young. But many others survived.

With each passing decade, pioneer colonists moved inland, up rivers, to the Appalachian Mountains. During much of the colonial period, British colonists thought of these mountains as a barrier to western movement. But, by the mid-1700s, American pioneers began crossing the mountains into a new frontier. It would become their new world.

The American Frontier

These brave, land-hungry pioneers were the first to spread across the lands that would become the United States. As they moved west, they established themselves on lands that had been kept natural by the American Indians. These lands were wilderness dotted by American Indian villages. This land was called the frontier. Throughout much of American history, there was a frontier. At times, there were several frontiers at once. None of these frontiers ever lasted very long.

Typically, when settlers reached any new western lands, they began a new frontier experience. But with each passing year, such settlers established their own style of civilization. They built their homes, trading posts, towns, schools, and churches. They wrote up local constitutions and laws to live by. Once a region became settled, it was no longer considered a frontier.

Making Their Way "West"

Historians define the term "frontier," when it relates to American history, as: the place lying between American civilization (the known) and what was seen by the settlers as wilderness (the unknown). Pioneers left the world they knew behind. They built new homes on lands that were new to them. They brought with them their ideas and experiences about schools, churches, and local government. They transplanted those ideas into their new frontier worlds. The result was a short-lived frontier period. Each frontier period usually might last not more than a few years. During this period, settlers, pioneers, and backwoodsmen lived between the known and the unknown. They came from a world that they knew. They entered regions that were strange to them. But once they arrived in these unknown, frontier places, they soon turned them into lands of their own.

Another important word used by historians when talking about the frontier is "the West." Pioneers who moved from the Atlantic Coast into new frontiers usually moved westward. But the term "the West," used to identify the frontier, is not a direction, but a place. With each new generation of settlers, the West moved. For someone living in Jamestown in 1630, the West was the Appalachian Mountains. For the 1750 pioneer, the West might be Kentucky, Ohio, or Tennessee. By 1850, those who traveled along the Oregon Trail thought of the West as Oregon or California. Just like the frontier, the West in American history was always moving.

Western Transportation Routes

As Americans moved west, they needed a way to get to the lands along the frontier. Travel during the American Colonial era was difficult. There were few roads in the Thirteen Colonies. Most of them did not connect from one colony to another. Also, there were many rivers running west to east, flowing into the

Atlantic Ocean. There were no bridges across any major river in the Thirteen Colonies. These rivers often cut off movement of Americans north to south. Sometimes, American Indian trails could be used. One was the Iroquois Trail in New York. It ran between the Hudson River and Lake Erie and followed the Mohawk

New roads and trails had to be hacked out of the wilderness.

River. Another was the Warriors' Path, which ran from North Carolina across the mountains into modern-day Ohio. These trails were narrow paths, often no wider than twelve or eighteen inches. They were not large enough for a settler's wagon.

To further open the way to the frontier, new roads and trails had to be hacked out of the wilderness. Two of these roads were built by British troops during the 1750s. At the time, the British and French were battling each other for control of the Ohio River Valley, an important frontier region. In 1755, British axmen cut out a road through western Virginia into western Pennsylvania. It was named after their commander, General Edward Braddock. The road reached then-French Fort Duquesne. Three years later, another British army created another frontier road across western Pennsylvania. It too was named for the army's general, John Forbes.

During the war, the British took control of Fort Duquesne, renaming it Fort Pitt, after one of their political leaders. This important frontier outpost was later renamed Pittsburgh. Its location at the headwaters of the Ohio River made it an important jumping-off place for pioneers headed west. Both Braddock's Road and Forbes's Road provided western settlers additional routes for travel. Thousands would use these roads through the following decades.

Many settlers used land routes, such as the Wilderness Trail and Forbes's Road, to get to the Trans-Appalachian frontier. Thousands poured into Kentucky and Tennessee, Ohio and western Pennsylvania. By the early 1780s, more than one hundred thousand pioneers had made these western places their homes.[1] With so many moving west, other roads were needed. During the 1790s, President George Washington was authorized by Congress to order the building of a road across Ohio. It would be called Zane's Trace. It became one of the earliest trails in Ohio that was not blazed by American Indians. Another road, the Lancaster Pike, was constructed between Lancaster, Pennsylvania, and Philadelphia.

Conestoga Wagon

Settlers used large, heavy Conestoga wagons on early American roads. The wagons were built by German immigrants who lived in the Conestoga Valley of Pennsylvania. These large, slow covered wagons carried freight before the coming of the railroads.

The Northwest Territory

During the 1770s and early 1780s, American colonists fought and won a war for independence against Great Britain. British law tried to limit the colonists' movement west of the Appalachian Mountains. But the new American government that was established after victory over the British encouraged such movement. More and more pioneers made their way into the Ohio Valley. Soon, this vast frontier region became settled. By the 1790s, Kentucky and Tennessee both became states. During the 1780s, the new United States Congress passed laws to help organize frontier settlement north of the Ohio River. This region was known as the Northwest Territory.

Congress passed one such law called the Land Ordinance of 1785. This act called for the survey of the Northwest Territory. This would help keep the sale of Ohio Valley land organized so pioneer land claims did not overlap. The ordinance called for the dividing of this territory into square townships, measuring six miles by six miles. Each township was divided into square-mile sections, thirty-six in all. Each township section was equal to 640 acres of land. The government then sold land to pioneers in 640-acre (one square mile) sections at one dollar an acre. The ordinance encouraged western migration. Soon, settlers were buying land in the Ohio Valley faster than it could be surveyed. A second act was the Northwest Ordinance of 1787. It allowed for the carving out of states in the Northwest Territory; eventually, Congress granted statehood to:

Northwest Territory

CANADA
(British)

Lake Superior

Virginia 1784

Lake Huron

Virginia and
New York

Lake Michigan

Lake Ontario

Lake Erie

Virginia, Massachusetts,
and New York 1784–1785

LOUISIANA
(Spanish)

Virginia, Connecticut, and
New York 1784–1786

Mississippi R.

Virginia and
New York 1784

Ohio R.

Missouri R.

Ohio R.

Virginia and
New York 1784

North Carolina and
New York 1784

Mississippi R.

South Carolina
and Georgia 1802

Disputed with Spain
until 1795; Georgia 1802

Vermont

Massachusetts

New
Hampshire

New
York

Massachusetts

Rhode
Island

Connecticut

Pennsylvania

New Jersey

Maryland

Delaware

Virginia

*Atlantic
Ocean*

North Carolina

South
Carolina

Georgia

N
W E
S

**Claims to Western Lands,
1784–1802**

Northwest Territory

This map shows the Northwest Territory and the states that laid claim to
various parts of it. Eventually, the territory was divided up into new states.

Ohio (1803), Indiana (1816), Illinois (1818), Michigan (1837), and Wisconsin (1848).

The National Road

People were moving west in greater numbers. More states were carved out of the Trans-Appalachian region. There was a great need for better roads. In 1802, Congress passed an act calling for the building of a western highway, the National Road (it would also be known as the Cumberland Road). It would be paid for by the federal government. This road would cut across Ohio, Indiana, and Illinois and would include parts of some roads that already existed. These included Braddock's Road and Zane's Trace. Unlike most roads in early nineteenth-century America, the National Road was a gravel-top route. It was paved with an inch of crushed stone and a layer of gravel laid on top. It was thirty feet wide. This allowed two large Conestoga wagons to pass one another. The road began in Maryland in 1808. It did not reach the eastern Ohio border for another ten years. Over the decades, the National Road stretched farther west. It reached Columbus, Ohio, in 1825; eastern Indiana in 1833; and eastern Illinois in 1850. A later leg of the road ran to the Mississippi River town of St. Louis.

The number of people in the Trans-Appalachian West mushroomed between 1795 and 1810. In 1795, approximately one hundred fifty thousand Americans lived west of the Appalachians. According to the federal census of 1810, that number rose to more than one million. Pioneers settled along the Great Lakes and the Ohio River, as well as other rivers including the Wabash, Kaskaskia, Illinois, and Alabama.[2]

River Highways

Roads such as the Lancaster Pike, Wilderness Trail, and the National Road certainly helped many pioneers reach the Trans-Appalachian West. But the settlers also traveled by river. Many used the Ohio River, as well as other rivers that flowed into it. Two types of western river craft were popular on these rivers. They were keelboats and flatboats. Keelboats were manned

A man dances as others watch on a journey on a flatboat down a river. This painting, called *Jolly Flatboatmen*, was done by George Caleb Bingham.

by professional crews. They used their boats to haul western freight for a fee. The boats were well built and included a keel and wooden ribbing. An average keel-boat was sixty to seventy feet long and included a sail.

Flatboats were first used in America on its western rivers, especially the Ohio. A flatboat was considered a temporary watercraft. One could be hammered together by anyone with basic carpentry skills. This type of river craft was not really a boat at all, but a big, wooden floating box. Flatboats were built in different sizes. A typical flatboat measured fifty feet long and about fourteen feet wide.[3] Flatboats were usually used by western farmers to get their produce to market.

Where western rivers did not flow, frontier

The Erie Canal

The most famous early American canal was the Erie Canal. It was built between 1817 and 1825. The canal ran nearly 350 miles from Albany to Buffalo, New York. After its opening, it became a popular means of hauling freight and delivering pioneers to the West.

By 1840, thousands of miles of canals were constructed in America. These canals were another transportation system for moving people and goods in and out of the rugged Trans-Appalachian region. However, the canal-building era in American history did not last long. Many such canals were soon replaced by two new types of American transportation: steamboats and the early railroad.

Americans supported the building of man-made waterways called canals. State governments funded most canal construction. Sometimes, the federal government paid for a canal to be built. Between 1820 and 1840, the American West experienced a canal-building craze. During the 1820s alone, states spent $26 million on canal construction. Half of this sum was paid by New York and New Jersey.

After designing the *Clermont*, Robert Fulton began working on a steam-powered warship called *Fulton the First*. However, he died in 1815 before its completion.

Steamboats on Western Rivers

The inventive American Robert Fulton is credited with designing and building the first practical and profitable steamboat in 1807. Fulton built his first steamboat, the *Clermont*, for use on an eastern river, the Hudson. The first steamboats built in the United States were used on eastern rivers. In only a few years, however, steamboats were in use on the Ohio and Mississippi rivers. The first western steamer was built by Nicholas Roosevelt in 1811. He launched his boat, the *New Orleans*, late that year. His steamboat made a trip down the Ohio River (the boat was built in Pittsburgh, near the river's headwaters) to the Mississippi River, then down to New Orleans. Roosevelt's voyage down these rivers brought steam power to the West.

Soon, the era of the river steamers was in full swing. By 1817, fourteen riverboats steamed up and down the Mississippi-Ohio system.[4] Two years later, the number had more than doubled. Steamboats could do things other boats could not. For one, their steam-powered paddle wheels allowed them to go upriver without using manpower. They also traveled faster

In this lithograph of St. Louis, Missouri, a number of steamboats are docked in the Mississippi river.

than any other boat on America's western rivers. A keelboat might travel twenty miles a day. A steamboat, as early as 1825, could cover more than one hundred miles along a river in a day.[5] Steamboats dramatically affected the amount of cargo carried along the Ohio and Mississippi rivers. In 1801, the value of the goods passing through New Orleans was about $4 million. By 1850, the amount had risen to nearly $100 million.[6]

Early Railroads in America

Steam power changed travel on America's rivers. It also changed land travel, as well. On July 4, 1828, the leading citizens of the city of Baltimore began building one of the earliest railroads in the United States: the Baltimore and Ohio Railroad (B&O). Charles Carroll, then the only living signer of the *Declaration of Independence*, was present at the dedication. He laid a stone to mark the site where construction on the B&O would begin. Originally, rail cars on the B&O were not powered by steam, but pulled by horses. But steam engines were introduced in just a few years.

This railroad was not the first in American history. But it was planned as a major route into the Trans-Appalachian West. The goal was for the B&O to be built through the Appalachian Mountains into the Ohio Valley. Construction dragged slowly on. Then, in 1842, the railroad finally reached Cumberland, Maryland. (Here, the National Road had been con-structed earlier.) A decade later, the B&O reached Wheeling, West Virginia. The early development of the

This early locomotive was used on the Baltimore and Ohio Railroad starting in 1832.

Baltimore and Ohio line made slow progress. But it managed to reach St. Louis in just four more years.[7]

Early railroad locomotives became the fastest means of transportation in America. According to historian Robert West Howard:

> Fulton's steamboat averaged only 4 3/4 miles an hour on its upstream runs between New York City and Albany. An ox team averaged 2 miles an hour, a canalboat 3 miles an hour, a stagecoach 6 to 8 miles an hour . . . [A] railroad train could travel 150 miles during a summer's day.[8]

Within just a few years, newly designed locomotives beat that speed hands down.

Beginning in the 1830s, the greatest American

designer of railroad locomotives was a Philadelphia jeweler named Matthias William Baldwin. He built his first "train" for a Philadelphia museum. It included a small engine and two cars that ran on a circular track. The little "toy" railroad became the museum's most popular attraction. But Baldwin continued building locomotives. Soon, he designed an engine that could travel nearly thirty miles an hour while pulling thirty tons.[9] With improvements, he doubled the speed of his locomotive to sixty miles an hour.[10] (Today, that engine is on display in the Franklin Institute Museum in Philadelphia.) Baldwin continued to work on engine designs until the 1860s. By 1866, the year he died, his company had built more than fifteen hundred railroad locomotives.[11]

One of the most important railroads to be built across the Ohio Country was the Illinois Central.

Railroading across the Trans-Appalachian region, from Ohio to Missouri, caught on quickly. By 1865, more than thirty-one thousand miles of railroad track had been laid east of the Mississippi River. That same year, there were more than three thousand miles of track west of the river, mostly in Missouri, Iowa, and Texas.[12] One of the most important railroads to be built across the Ohio Country was the Illinois Central. Chartered in 1850, the railroad attracted hundreds of thousands of settlers into Illinois. Between 1850 and 1860, the population of Illinois doubled. An additional six hundred thousand people became Illinois residents during the 1860s.[13]

The pattern was the same throughout the Trans-Appalachian West. Ohio was home to nearly one million people by 1830 and another five hundred thousand ten years later. That same year, Michigan's population passed the two hundred thousand mark. Illinois's population more than tripled between 1830 and 1840 to more than 475,000 residents. In 1840, more than one of every four Americans (out of a total population greater than 17 million) lived west of the Appalachian Mountains.[14]

Already, the Trans-Appalachian frontier was closed. Ohio and Indiana were largely settled by the 1820s. Much of the rest of the Old Northwest—Illinois, southern Michigan, and southern Wisconsin—were settled a decade later. By 1850, the South, from Tennessee to Mississippi and Alabama, had also slipped out of its frontier era.[15] Most of the pioneer log cabins were gone, replaced by more substantial houses. Villages and towns had become important American cities. Among the most important were Cincinnati, Louisville, Chicago, Nashville, and St. Louis. There was still a frontier in America, but it had moved farther west.

Into the West

By the opening of the nineteenth century, the western boundary of the United States had long passed beyond the Appalachian Mountains. Hundreds of thousands of pioneers had spread out across the lands of the Ohio Country. They were living in the Kentucky Bluegrass region, Tennessee, and the Old Southwest (modern-day states of Mississippi and Alabama). With the arrival of a new century, the American mission to spread west took on a new view. Some Americans began to focus on the unknown—lands west of the Mississippi River. Among those promoting that vision was the president of the United States, Thomas Jefferson.

Following the American Revolution, the defeated British Crown ceded land to the United States. It stretched from the Atlantic Ocean to the Mississippi River and from the Great Lakes to Florida. The newly independent America began to create a new government for itself. Its leaders realized their new country was surrounded by lands held by European powers. To the north was British-controlled Canada. To the south was Spanish-held Florida. West of the Mississippi River were the vast colonial landholdings of the

Spanish Crown. With Europeans at its very back door, the new American republic sometimes felt threatened.

In 1802, one such threat took place. The Spanish government ordered the port of New Orleans closed to American river traffic. But when the American protest became loud and strong, the Spanish soon backed off. Then, the following year, Napoléon Bonaparte, ruler of France, forced the Spanish to cede the immense territory of Louisiana to the French. The move concerned western Americans. By the early 1800s, New Orleans annually received between four hundred and seven hundred flatboats carrying American farm produce.[1] Frontier families relied on New Orleans for getting their goods to market.

Thomas Jefferson nearly doubled the size of the United States when he approved the purchase of the Louisiana Territory. This painting of him was done by John Trumbull.

With the closing of the port, President Jefferson began to take bold steps. He would not watch helplessly as Napoleon began building up a French empire in the New World. To share the Mississippi with the French would pose too much of a threat. Jefferson soon sent former Virginia governor James Madison to Paris. He was to negotiate for the purchase of New Orleans from the French. When he arrived in the spring of 1803, he and his colleague, Robert Livingston, were soon surprised. The French asked if the Americans were interested in buying the entire region of Louisiana. Burdened by years of war, Napoleon desperately needed money and had given up his dream of restoring French power in North America. Before year's end, the French government sold the vast territory to the American government for $15 million. The purchase more than doubled the size of the United States. It clearly protected American trade on the Mississippi River. The port of New Orleans was now American territory.

The Lewis and Clark Expedition

Even before purchasing Louisiana, President Jefferson had decided to send a group of U.S. Army explorers west of the Mississippi. Much of the vast Great Plains and Rocky Mountain region was a great unknown to Americans. Jefferson was extremely interested in America getting into the western fur trade. This western market was generally dominated by British, French, Spanish, and even Russian trappers. But now Louisiana was American territory. Such an exploration was even more important.

Jefferson chose his personal secretary, twenty-nine-year-old Meriwether Lewis, and Lewis's former army commander, William Clark, to lead the expedition. Captains Lewis and Clark selected nearly three dozen men to join their great western trek. The party gathered near St. Louis in the fall of 1803. They headed up the Missouri River the following April. The men of this expedition, called the Corps of Discovery, would spend the next twenty-eight months facing extraordinary hardship.

With the help of an American Indian woman named Sacagawea and another Shoshone Indian guide, the men made their way up the entire length of the Missouri River. They crossed the Rocky Mountains and finally reached the Pacific Ocean by the fall of 1805. Lewis and Clark returned to St. Louis in the fall of 1806. They brought back with them much information and knowledge about the Trans-Mississippi West. Clark had drawn up an accurate map of the lands the Corps crossed. He and Lewis had met with the leaders of more than fifty Indian tribes. These men had seen firsthand what no other American had ever witnessed: the vastness of the Rocky Mountains and the wealth they held in beaver fur.

Meriwether Lewis (top) and William Clark (bottom) had to deal with both friendly and unfriendly American Indians during their trip of discovery.

Western Fur Trade

Few things lured Americans into the Far West region of the

Rocky Mountains over the next generation like the fur trade. In the eastern United States and Europe, thick, soft beaver fur was very popular because it was made into men's hats, women's capes and collars, and other types of clothing during the early nineteenth century. These fashions

Zebulon Pike

As Lewis and Clark moved up the Missouri River, another army expedition explored the upper Mississippi River. Led by Zebulon Pike in 1805, the party failed to correctly identify the true source of the great American river.

drove the price for beaver skins up. With the demand for beaver high, profits inspired thousands of fur trappers in the West. Beaver could be found in abundance, living along the northern Great Plains and the Rocky Mountains.[2] But fur trapping and trading needed a special type of westerner. These men, called mountain men, lived rugged lives, working in the upland streams. As mountain men tromped across the unknown, uncharted lands of the northern and southern Rockies, they discovered where the rivers flowed and how high the mountains stood. They found passes through the Rockies where the next generation of Americans could cross the massive western barrier into the next American West.

New Western Trails

Earlier generations of Americans had used the various Indian trails and wilderness roads to cross the Appalachian Mountains. In the same way, important trails developed across the Trans-Mississippi West. By

The Rocky Mountains were a harsh terrain for even the most experienced explorers to cross. This was especially true during the winter months.

the 1820s, Americans reached out to trade with the Mexicans in Santa Fe. (Mexico had gained its independence from Spain in 1821.) This international exchange of goods helped develop a trade road that linked Missouri towns with the Mexican capital of New Mexico, Santa Fe. The trail was little more than a widely used wagon path. It ran from Independence, Missouri, across the flat prairie lands of modern-day Kansas to the Arkansas River. The trail then followed the river to Bent's Fort, on the Upper Arkansas. The route then cut southwest to Santa Fe. Some traders used a shorter route, cutting southwest across Kansas, following the Cimmaron River, then turning south to Santa Fe. This leg was more treacherous and American Indian attacks more common, especially by the Pawnee and Comanche.

This important trade route across the Trans-Mississippi West resulted in profits for the Mexicans and Americans. In 1822, trade along the trail amounted to only fifteen thousand dollars. Nine years later, the amount had jumped to two hundred fifty thousand dollars. By 1843, hundreds of Americans were using the Santa Fe Trail and the value of the goods traded equaled a half million dollars.[3] The trade

Wagon Train

The typical wagon train on the Santa Fe Trail often included as many as one hundred wagons. These wagons were the same Conestogas that had been so popular back east. Missouri traders usually delivered manufactured goods to Santa Fe. In exchange, they returned with Spanish silver dollars and mules. So many mules were introduced into Missouri that they became known as the Missouri Mules.

finally ended in the 1840s with the outbreak of the Mexican War between the United States and Mexico. When that war was over, much of the Southwest became American territory. During an earlier generation, Americans had already reached the rich farmlands of east Texas. Between 1820 and 1845, approximately eighty thousand Americans had pushed their way into the Southwest. The majority made their homes in Texas.[4]

The Oregon and California Trails

But of all the far western trail routes, none was more important than the Oregon Trail and its famous detour, the California Cutoff. Throughout the early decades of the 1800s, the vast Oregon Country (largely the modern-day states of Washington, Oregon, and Idaho) was a disputed region. The British, Spanish, Russians, and the Americans all claimed it. The land was rich with timber, valuable furs, and untilled farmlands. The land was home to many American Indians, but few other permanent residents. Each nation's claim was based on the landing of one of its ship's captains or some earlier exploration, such as the Lewis and Clark expedition.

The future of Oregon remained cloudy until the 1840s. By then, Americans decided it should be theirs. Following the War of 1812, which the United States fought with Great Britain, the nation turned toward the West with renewed interest. Many thought of the United States as a nation established by God and blessed with a bright future. They felt that the great American republic would spread across the Mississippi. Maybe it would stretch clear to the Pacific Ocean, as Lewis and Clark had already done. Some people believed that it was America's future, its true destiny, to establish its borders from one ocean to the next, covering all of North America. As Americans did so, they would be spreading the benefits of democracy. This view of America became known as Manifest Destiny. (The word "manifest," here, means obvious or clear.)

The term was first used by an easterner named John L. O'Sullivan. He wrote in 1845 that the move to the West would be the "fulfillment of our manifest destiny to overspread the content allotted by Providence [God's Will] for the free development of our yearly multiplying millions."[5] Newspapers published editorials in support of this belief. Ministers preached it from their pulpits. Politicians gave long speeches citing why the lands of the West should all be American territory. One such political leader was Senator Stephen Douglas of Illinois. In an 1845 speech, he declared "our federal system is admirably adapted to the whole continent."[6] Some opposed the drive to expand America's borders. When Democrats rallied to annex Oregon in 1846, Whig congressmen fought against it. They called for the U.S. government to divide Oregon and "share" it with the British.

The Oregon Trail was one of the longest continuous trails on the American landscape. It ran from Missouri to Oregon, a sometimes difficult road that

As a congressman and later a senator, Stephen A. Douglas pushed for a transcontinental railroad.

extended its dusty course for more than twenty-four hundred miles.[7]

Bison and, later, American Indians had first established portions of the trail hundreds of years earlier. Mountain men were among the first Americans to use the trail to reach the destinations in the Rockies. Their discovery of South Pass would provide a route through the Rockies for wagon trains to follow.

But mountain men traveling west on the Oregon Trail was one thing. For the trail to be followed by women and children was considered too difficult and too dangerous. Nevertheless, in 1831, a Massachusetts schoolteacher named Hall Jackson Kelley organized a society for settling the Oregon Country. He wanted to establish a settlement of New Englanders in the far distant reaches of Oregon, along the mighty Columbia River. The following year, a small party of New England residents signed on with an excited businessman and Oregon promoter, Nathaniel Wyeth, to make the trip. That spring, Wyeth's small party reached St. Louis and began their float up the Missouri River. At Independence, Missouri, the emigrant group joined the annual trading expedition of the Rocky Mountain

Fur Company. The trip proved quite difficult, and some of Wyeth's party turned around in modern-day Wyoming, bound for home. But Wyeth and eleven of his companions completed their journey.

Despite the challenges facing pioneers traveling the Oregon Trail, thousands joined wagon trains. Some were driven west by unemployment and economic hard times. But many were midwestern farmers seeking better opportunities in Oregon. The cost of outfitting a wagon was expensive. Many poor people simply could not afford the trip along the two-thousand-mile-long trail. Some went west for other, personal reasons. Attempting to convince his family to follow him west, one would-be pioneer, a farmer named Peter Burnett, told them:

> Out in Oregon I can get me a square mile of land. And a quarter section for each of you all. Dad burn me, I am done with this country, Winters it's frost and snow to freeze a body; summers the overflow from Old Muddy [the Mississippi River] drowns half my acres.[8]

West they went. The difficulties of the trail proved as real as the problems these easterners moving west left behind. The trail required six months of travel from Independence to Oregon's Columbia River. To make the long, hard trek, a family had to take a small wagon, one much smaller than a Conestoga. The western trail was too rugged and the mountain passes too steep and twisting for the popular Dutch freight wagon. This new type of wagon's bed held everything

A man and a woman sit in an original prairie schooner. This wagon was used in Buffalo Bill's Wild West Show in the 1880s.

the family wanted to take to their new home in Oregon, including their food supply—all six months' worth. These western wagons, often called prairie schooners by the Oregon pioneers, weighed one thousand pounds empty. Fully loaded with a family's household trunk, they might weigh an additional fifteen hundred pounds. Often, families had to throw out some of their belongings to lighten their wagonloads while crossing difficult western terrain.

The Oregon Trail delivered hundreds of thousands of emigrants to Oregon and California. The United States was moving farther and farther west. As the emigrants moved, they established new frontiers in these new, unsettled lands.

"God Preserve This Whole Country"

As Americans moved west along the Oregon Trail by the 1840s, the lands of the West looked destined for American occupation. The presidential election of 1844 brought James K. Polk, of Tennessee, to the White House. Polk campaigned on promises to annex the Oregon Country as American territory, as well as Texas, which was part of Mexico. Following his election, he was able to negotiate a treaty with the British. It called for the British to cede control of Oregon south of the 49th parallel. As for Texas, Congress voted statehood for the former Mexican republic in 1845, between Polk's election and his inauguration. These exchanges of land ownership, claim, and control left only the Southwest still in foreign hands.

But, during Polk's term, the United States went to war with Mexico. When the United States annexed Texas, the Mexican government refused to accept the

Under President James K. Polk, the United States greatly expanded its borders by acquiring Texas, California, the Oregon Territory, and what would become New Mexico and Arizona.

decision. (The Mexican Congress had never ratified the 1836 Treaty of Velasco under which Mexican president and general Antonio López de Santa Anna had agreed to Texas independence.) President Polk further pushed for war. He dispatched American troops to occupy the northern bank of the Rio Grande in June 1845. The Mexican government had never considered the Rio Grande as the southern border of Texas. They had always claimed the Nueces River as the legal border. With American forces along the Rio Grande, they were, according to the Mexican government, trespassing on Mexican soil. By April 1846, the two sides had engaged in a battle, which led to the outbreak of the Mexican-American War.

The war lasted less than eighteen months and was over by September 1847. American forces won nearly every battle and eventually marched into Mexico City itself. Six months later, both sides agreed to the Treaty of Guadalupe Hidalgo. Under this agreement, the

United States paid Mexico $15 million. In exchange, the United States received the vast expanse of Mexico's northern land claims above the Rio Grande. This large region included modern-day California, Arizona, New Mexico, Utah, Nevada, and parts of southern Colorado and western Texas.

With this agreement, the United States gained control of the last remaining block of western territory. Throughout the first half of the nineteenth century, the United States had amassed much land west of the Mississippi River. These lands included the Louisiana Purchase, Texas, the Oregon Country, and finally

During the Mexican War, General Zachary Taylor (right, in this lithograph by James S. Baillie) led American troops to victory at the Battle of Buena Vista. The United States would go on to win the war and much of Mexico's territory.

the Mexican Cession. America stretched from the Mississippi to the Pacific Coast. Gone were the European challenges that held back earlier migration into the West, including the French, British, Spanish, and Russians. The lands from the Atlantic to the Pacific and from the Great Lakes to the Gulf of Mexico were now entirely American. Hundreds of millions of square miles of western territory were open for development and settlement.

Early Plans for a Transcontinental Railroad

Even as early as the 1840s, some Americans were beginning to dream of a railroad spanning the continent from sea to sea. All other forms of western travel—steamboat, stagecoach, wagon train—seemed too slow for the West. It seemed so because the Great Plains and the Rocky Mountain chain to their west seemed endless. Moving along the various western trails and rivers trying to cover the great expanses of territory required weeks of travel at a minimum. All westerners who had experienced the speed and efficiency of eastern railroads knew the immediate answer for faster, western travel; it lay in the western expansion of steam and rail.

One of the first Americans to dream about such a western rail line was Asa Whitney. He was a New York City merchant and trader. He had connections to Asian markets by sea. By the mid-1840s, Whitney had developed an imaginary track running from the Great Lakes to the mouth of the Columbia River. From there, great clipper ships could sail back and forth to Asian markets. With great enthusiasm, Whitney made a trip through the region where the eastern portion of his proposed railroad would run. This convinced him even more that such a railroad was necessary.

In 1845, he sent a proposal to Congress in support of his transcontinental rail route. Whitney's proposal called for the U.S. government to grant him a giant ribbon of western land. It would extend sixty miles wide from north to south and run from the Mississippi River and Iowa Territory to the great Columbia River Valley. Such a grant would include 75 million acres of western land! His railroad's western terminus was to be Chicago. Working to Whitney's advantage in this proposal was that, in 1845, Mexico still controlled the southwestern lands from California to New Mexico, eliminating, at that time, the possibility of a southern route for any railroad across the West.

Whitney, working through a federal commission, was responsible for selling this land to would-be farmers and homesteaders, as well as to other developers. These would include lumber companies and mining interests. His proposed Lake Michigan-Oregon Railway was to be built from the monies generated through public land sales and by granting companies

Clipper Ships

Clipper ships were the fastest ships of the early nineteenth century. These great heavy-masted, yet very sleek, ships traveled across oceans and delivered cargoes of exotic Chinese silks, teak woods, spices, and teas to American ports as distant as Boston and New York.

lumber and mineral rights. "Here we stand forever," stated Whitney's railroad proposal. "We reach out one hand to all Asia and the other to all Europe, willing for all to enjoy the great blessings we possess, claiming free intercourse and exchange of commodities with all."[1]

Whitney's proposal met with controversy and opposition from the start. It all seemed too much to many politicians. It would require too much construction and too much land. Above all, most congressmen were not convinced such a rail line could be built at all. The American West was a place of difficult terrain. It was home to immense mountains; endless, grassy plains; and dry, arid desert lands.

Four years later, a popular Missouri politician, U.S. Senator Thomas Hart Benton, proposed an alternative route. It was to run from California's San Francisco to his home state, with its eastern end point in St. Louis. This proposal was known as the Pacific Railroad Bill.

Soon, other proposals were being made by other congressmen and senators. Each called for cities in their home states to serve as the eastern hub of a proposed western railroad. These included Milwaukee, Chicago, Memphis, Vicksburg, even New Orleans. A lively rivalry developed between competing states. Each knew the importance such a rail line would mean for the economy and future of their state. One rivalry pitted northern states and southern states against one another. Southerners expected a southern rail line to help them extend slavery farther West. Northerners did not intend to allow such expansion to encourage western slavery.

The California Gold Rush

As the debate over a proposed route across the West wore on, western events further complicated matters. In January 1848, James Marshall, a carpenter, was working on a sawmill on the American River on a northern California ranch that was owned by a Swiss immigrant named John Sutter. Marshall noticed several glimmering rocks in the tailrace and thought they might be gold. When he turned the samples over to Sutter, tests were made to determine if the rocks were, indeed, gold. They were. Sutter forced Marshall to promise to keep their secret quiet. But word soon spread of gold discoveries along the American River, in the Sacramento Valley. Word reached San Francisco by March 15, 1848. Within a year, northern California was overrun with gold seekers.[2]

The secret of gold in northern California was out. In the meantime, the United States and Mexico signed a mutual treaty that handed California over to the Americans. Suddenly, California was American territory. It was also the site of one of the most extensive gold rushes in American history. For supporters of Manifest Destiny, the gold discoveries were God's invitation for Americans to consider California as their own. As one American promoter wrote:

> Why, Sir, did God preserve this whole country more than a century after its discovery for the English,

turning the foot of the Spaniard to the sunny region of the tropics? . . . In fine, why were the immense treasures of California hidden from the world until she was annexed to this Republic? And tell me, if anyone can, why it was that the title deed of transference had no sooner passed into our hands than she gave up her mighty secret and unlocked her golden gates?[3]

People began heading to California by the thousands. By the summer of 1848, the non-American Indian population in California was two thousand. By October, it was five thousand and, by year's end, it stood at eight thousand. People came from everywhere—Mexico, South America, even Hawaii. But mostly they came from the eastern United States. And the trickling numbers of 1848 would become a flood by 1849.[4] They came into San Francisco Bay by sailing ship, having experienced the six-month, eighteen-thousand-mile voyage from New England to northern California. By December 1849, at least forty thousand prospectors were at work seeking their fortunes along rivers in northern California.[5] The following year would deliver twice that number, including fifty thousand by land and thirty-five thousand by sea.[6] Few miners ever struck it rich in the gold diggings. But the California Gold Rush of 1849 changed the course of the history of the Far West. So many people had moved to the gold camps, their numbers allowed California to become an American state by 1850.

Far Western Transportation

The Gold Rush in California pushed American migration to the western-most edge of the North American continent. Americans had taken nearly two centuries to move from their coastal colonies to the eastern banks of the Mississippi. During the first two decades of the nineteenth century, they had pushed out onto the western prairies from Minnesota to Arkansas. Then came the lure of gold in California and rich farming land in the Oregon Country. Americans had crossed the Great Plains and the Rocky Mountains and reached the Far West in just one generation. (They had not settled the Great Plains or Rocky Mountain region yet, however.) This settlement pattern left a great gulf between eastern settlements and the gold camps and Oregon farms. Once more, the great need arose to develop transportation systems to link the two regions.

Heavy wagons still served westerners who needed to haul cargoes of freight to mining camps, western military forts, and other settlement sites. Freight wagon companies sprang up across the Far West. They provided regular and reliable freight transport. But it was never about speed. Something else was needed to carry passengers across the West faster. A stagecoach

Isthmus of Panama

Almost seven thousand gold prospectors crossed the Isthmus of Panama in 1849 to reach California faster than sailing around South America. However, they ran a high risk of contracting yellow fever and malaria. Many died. By the early 1850s, a railroad line was built across the Isthmus to deliver miners and other travelers from coast to coast faster and safer.

line was opened in 1850 between Independence, Missouri, and Salt Lake City, Utah. The following year, the line was extended to California. But the line was poorly operated. Winter weather shut it down completely. Then, in 1858, a new western stagecoach line was established. It was popularly known as the Butterfield Overland Express, after one of its original investors, John Butterfield. Butterfield was from New York and was himself a stagecoach driver. Through shrewd investments, Butterfield soon owned stakes in several transportation systems in America. These included eastern stage lines and canal packet boats.

The federal government granted Butterfield and his fellow investors the contract to build a stagecoach line across the West in 1857. The government paid six hundred thousand dollars for the new stage line to deliver the mails semiweekly in both directions. The Butterfield Line ran from St. Louis, Missouri, along a route that ran southwest to El Paso, Texas. It continued west across modern-day New Mexico and Arizona. Finally, the route arched northwest toward Los Angeles, then northern California until it reached Sacramento.

By the spring of 1858, Butterfield had overseen the construction of 141 stagecoach stations. His workers had built bridges to ford rivers. He owned fifteen hundred mules and horses. He purchased two hundred fifty stagecoaches from the Abbott and Downing Stagecoach Company of Concord, New Hampshire.[7] These "Concord" stages became the standard stagecoach used across the West. They were well built and handcrafted. Each coach body rested on leather straps to help cushion the bumpy ride across the western frontier. The stage line ran two thousand miles long. A trip by stagecoach took nearly four weeks. This was much faster than a ship passage around South America or by wagon along the Oregon and California trails.

Despite early successes, the Butterfield Stage Line did not last many years. When the Civil War opened in 1861, the southern route was abandoned. A new line was opened from St. Joseph to Salt Lake City, then on to Folsom, California. The line—called the Overland Stage Line—was established by the firm of Russell, Majors, & Waddell. Spur lines were added to the main

In the mid-1800s, many different companies operated stagecoach lines throughout the country. The coach pictured above was part of the "Phoenix Line," which ran between Baltimore, Maryland, and Washington, D.C.

stagecoach line. By 1866, the line's owner, Ben Holladay, was operating five thousand miles of western stage mileage. That year, he sold his business to Wells, Fargo & Company, one of the most famous western stagecoach companies.

During these same years, a unique and faster way to deliver the mail across the West began operation. In 1860, the company of Russell, Majors, & Waddell established the Pony Express. The system relied on lightweight, young riders to carry the mail between St. Joseph and Sacramento, California. Speed was important. The line included a series of "stations" where a rider could switch to a fresh horse. Delivery of a letter along the Pony Express was expensive—ten dollars an ounce.[8] The line was costly to operate. By 1861, it went out of business. It was replaced by a new telegraph line that stretched along the full length of the Pony Express route.

Western Cattle Industry

Through the years, more and more people spread across the Great Plains and the Far West. With this, there was a growing need to develop the West's natural resources. Two abundant resources found in the West were cattle and mineral wealth, especially silver and gold. Two industries, then, developed as major parts of the western economy—the cattle business and large-scale mining.

During the Civil War, the demand for western beef soared. For hundreds of years, Spanish herds had been

The Pony Express rider in this painting by William Henry Jackson is trying to escape American Indians. Riders were sometimes attacked by Indians who thought that Americans were ruining their land and killing the buffalo, an important source of food and clothing for the Indians.

raised on Spanish and later Mexican ranches across the Southwest. As cattle wandered away from various herds, the West was eventually home to millions of unclaimed animals. By 1860, in Texas alone, an estimated 5 million head of longhorn cattle roamed across the region's southern grasslands. In the spring of 1866, Illinois-born cattleman Joseph G. McCoy encouraged western cattle herders to drive these free cattle north from Texas to Abilene, Kansas. There, they could be loaded onto railroad cars for shipment. The following year, cowboys rounded up tens of thousands

In this painting by Charles Russell, a cowboy tries to tame a bucking horse. A cowboy's main job was to drive cattle over miles of prairie land.

of longhorns and drove them up through Texas and Oklahoma to Abilene. That summer, thirty-five thousand head reached the stockyards McCoy had built there. During the years that followed, an extensive cattle industry developed in the West.

From 1866 to 1885, cowhands annually rounded up herds of Texas cattle and drove them north on the "Long Drive." It was difficult work, but the rewards could be great. In 1868, a Texas cowman might invest five thousand dollars in a herd of six hundred steers, drive them north, and sell them in Abilene for more than sixteen thousand dollars, netting him a profit of eleven thousand dollars.[9] In 1871 alone, cowboys drove nearly two hundred thousand head of cattle to Abilene. Ten years later, Dodge City, Kansas, another cowtown, took in more than two hundred thousand head.[10]

As for mining, its lure of quick riches began to fade by the late 1850s. By then, the valuable metals near the earth's surface had been collected by prospectors. Western miners were forced to invest in heavy equipment operations and dig mines deep underground. Hard-rock mining operations cropped up across the West. Much of this mining took place in Colorado, Idaho, Montana, Nevada, and California. Other mining sites of less importance included those in Arizona, Washington Territory, and the Dakotas. Miners faced many difficulties working the shafts deep underground. Sometimes they extended a mile down. Hard-rock mining could produce high profits for mining investors.

Planning America's Railroad

Throughout the 1850s, Congress debated over the route for a transcontinental railroad. In the meantime, railroad technology continued to improve. Each new innovation made the construction of a long, western rail line more practical and feasible. By March 1853, Congress approved the Pacific Railroad Survey Act. It set aside $150,000 for the surveying of several possible routes for a western rail line. Soon, U.S. Army topographical engineers were scrambling across the West. They surveyed at least five possible central and southern routes. Not to be left out, the governor of the Washington Territory, Isaac Stevens, ordered another survey for a possible far northern route.

In Search of a Viable Western Route

The routes surveyed all ran east to west, but across different places through the Great Plains. The most northern route would run from St. Paul, Minnesota, across the Northern Plains to Vancouver, Canada. The second proposed route would cross the Plains from

Council Bluffs, Iowa, following the Oregon and Mormon trails along the 41st and 42nd parallels through South Pass to Benicia, California.

A third route would begin in Westport, Missouri, and follow the 38th and 39th parallels to San Francisco. The fourth surveyed route began its line at Fort Smith, Arkansas. It would follow the Santa Fe Trail, then western Spanish trails to California. Surveyors decided this route would be the most expensive to construct. The fifth route would follow the 32nd parallel out of Fulton, Arkansas, to San Pedro, California. Its estimated cost was the lowest of the five proposed routes, tagged at $69 million. (The Fort Smith line was estimated to cost $100 million more than that.)[1] This line would also be the shortest to construct. In addition, snows would rarely ever be a problem on a route running that far south.

By the early 1850s, a southern route for a

The Mormon Trail

The Mormon Trail was the western route followed by the religious group known as the Church of Jesus Christ of Latter-Day Saints. Strangers to the group called them the Mormons. The Mormons used the trail beginning in the 1840s to reach modern-day Utah where they established a colony. The trail largely followed the eastern half of the Oregon Trail through South Pass in the Rocky Mountains. From there, it cut southwest into the Valley of the Great Salt Lake.

transcontinental line was thought to be possible. The same year the Pacific Railroad Survey Act was passed, an American negotiator, James Gadsden, sat down again with representatives of Mexico. They discussed the possibility of Mexico ceding additional land to the United States. At stake was a forty-five-thousand-square-mile tract lying south of the Gila River and

Davis helped sell the need for the purchase of this desert region.

east to El Paso del Norte. The purchase was almost entirely inspired by the South. In 1853, the nation's secretary of war was a Mississippian named Jefferson Davis. (Less than ten year later, Davis would become the first president of the Confederate States of America during the Civil War.) Gadsden was a rail-road promoter from Charleston, South Carolina. These two, as well as other southerners, believed a rail line should be constructed connecting the Pacific and the South. U.S. Army surveys had already hinted that the best route for such a rail line should run through the Rio Grande Valley. Davis helped sell the need for the purchase of this desert region and its "dire importance to national defense."[2]

But others did not want a southern route. Stephen Douglas, now an Illinois senator, proposed legislation to establish the central-western territories of Nebraska and Kansas. This would help promote a central rail route, with Chicago as its terminus. In 1854, Douglas introduced his Kansas-Nebraska Bill. But southerners would not support a northern route. Also, the Douglas proposal did not expressly open up these territories for slavery. This presented another reason for southerners not to support the bill. Soon, in fact, the burning issue of slavery overshadowed all proposals for a western railroad. A national depression struck in 1857. Soon, most talk of western railroad construction ground to a halt.

Railroad Construction in California

The 1850s slipped by, and Congress made no other important decisions about where to build a transcontinental rail line across the West. In the meantime, railroad construction was taking place in California. (As late as 1858, no track was laid west of Kansas, except in California.) As early as 1855, a twenty-one-mile-long rail line—the Sacramento Valley Railroad—had been completed.

The 1860 presidential election turned America's interest once again to construction of a transcontinental railroad. At the Republican National Convention, party delegates added a pro-railroad plank to their platform. They declared that "a Railroad to the pacific Ocean is imperatively demanded by the interests of the whole country."[3] Soon, the proposed line was an election issue. But the overriding issue was slavery and talk of the Southern states leaving the Union. For decades, Northern and Southern interests had debated whether slavery should expand west of the Mississippi River. Then, the Republican candidate, Abraham Lincoln of Illinois, was elected. Immediately, Southern states began taking steps to leave the Union. (Lincoln had made it clear he was opposed to the spread of slavery into the West.) By the spring of 1861, several Southern states had formed the Confederate States of America. The next four years would witness a bloody civil war between the North and the South. With the country

With Congress's approval, President Lincoln signed the Pacific Railroad Act on July 1, 1862.

divided and the southern states no longer in the Union, it was clear that a transcontinental railroad would not follow a southern route. In fact, with the war on, "Congress had an enhanced interest in advancing the cause of a pacific railroad, to counteract the efforts of the Confederacy to detach the territories and western states from the Union."[4]

The Southern states were no longer in Congress to demand a southern route for the railroad across the West. This freed Congress to select a route that Northern states could accept. The route out of Council Bluffs was chosen. The selected road followed the Oregon and Mormon trails. The route was called the Platte Valley Route. It paralleled the Nebraska portions of the Platte River. With Congress's approval, President Lincoln signed the

Pacific Railroad Act on July 1, 1862. The country was then into its second year of the Civil War.

The newly signed law was complicated. It called for a railroad line to be constructed by two railroads, the Central Pacific and the Union Pacific. Both lines were new railroad companies formed to build the transcontinental rail line. The construction project was so big, no single rail company in the world was large enough to build the line. The Central Pacific would begin building in California toward the East. The Union Pacific would lay track starting in Nebraska and build toward California. Somewhere, out in the trackless wilderness of the Far West, the two railroads would link up. No one knew how long it would take or where the railroads would meet. The 1862 law did not specify where the two lines would connect.

The terms granted the railroads were generous. The railroad act granted both railroads a four-hundred-foot-wide right-of-way. This meant they would own land extending four hundred feet on both sides of the line of track. The companies could use all the timber, stone, and earth along the right-of-way for construction. The rail companies were granted additional lands as well. They received five alternate land sections for each mile of track built. These sections, however, were granted in a checkerboard pattern with every other section situated on the opposite side of the rail line. This kept the railroads from owning one long strip of land along their portion of the rail route. This meant that, for every mile of track constructed, the railroads would receive sixty-four hundred acres of public land. It would all be located within ten miles of their tracks. The railroads were not granted the mineral rights on these lands, however.

Building the long railroad line would take lots of money. The government loaned federal treasury bonds to the railroads for each mile of track constructed. These bonds could then be sold to the public. Repayment on the bonds was set at thirty years. The federal government would make interest payments to investors. These bonds were issued per mile of track built. The amount issued depended on the type of terrain covered. For construction of a mile of track across flat terrain, the railroads received sixteen thousand dollars in bonds. Through the foothills of the Rockies and the Sierra Nevada range, the government paid thirty-two thousand dollars per mile. For construction through the difficult mountain country, forty-eight thousand dollars was paid per mile.[5]

Bonds

Congress loaned $50 million in interest-free bonds to the railroads. The government also gave them 20 million acres of land.

Railroad Leadership

The construction of the proposed railroad line would be a huge undertaking. The two rail companies would have extraordinary responsibilities. These included arranging financing, organizing construction crews, overseeing the costs of surveying, grading, and building the line. The men who took the leadership of the Central Pacific and

Union Pacific would need to be extraordinary individuals. The Central Pacific was led by a foursome of organizers: Leland Stanford, Collis P. Huntington, Charles Crocker, and Mark Hopkins. All four men had gone to California following the 1849 Gold Rush. They were lured into taking the reins of the Central Pacific. They became interested after hearing a railroad promoter speak in November 1860 at the St. Joseph Hotel in Sacramento.

The promoter was a Connecticut engineer named Theodore Judah. He first arrived in California in the spring of 1854. He had been hired to survey and build the Sacramento Valley Railroad. This short line ran from Sacramento to Folsom, just west of the Sierra Nevadas, where the railroad would later service the gold seekers along the American River. The line had been completed the following year. Judah remained in California. He was interested in a future transcontinental line connecting to his railroad. He studied the mountains in search of a viable route through them. At that time, railroad locomotives could pull trains up a mountain grade no steeper than 110 feet per mile. Was such a grade even possible through the steep, rocky Sierra Nevadas?

Through the summer of 1860, Judah tromped across the Sierra Nevada range. He was looking for a viable route. A merchant in one of the local mining towns told Judah of a possible route along the American River into the Sierras. By summer's end, he had spent weeks hiking across the range, sleeping outdoors, and surveying. The route would cross through Donner Pass, near the Truckee River. It was here that a party of pioneers had become trapped in snows along the California Trail in 1846–1847. Through the long winter, some of those caught in the mountains turned to cannibalism.

Judah was able to establish a route that never created a grade of more than 105 feet per mile. But the route would require much excavation and blasting out of tunnels. Workers would have to cut a cliff-side shelf where trains would move along a sheer drop.

Armed with his survey maps, Judah invited the public to a meeting at the St. Joseph Hotel. Among the people there were Stanford, Huntington, Crocker, and Hopkins. They were all businessmen and merchants in Sacramento. Stanford was a wholesale grocer. Crocker sold dry goods. Huntington and Hopkins were partners in a hardware business. They were interested in Judah's presentation. Soon, they and three other investors provided thirty-five thousand dollars of their own money to pay Judah to complete a more extensive survey.

Judah completed his new

Leland Stanford

Leland Stanford was president of the Central Pacific Railroad from 1861 until his death in 1893. In 1884, he and other railroad leaders united all California railroads under the name Southern Pacific. He also served as president of that company from 1884 to 1890.

Stanford founded a university in California. He named it Stanford University after his son, Leland Stanford, Jr., who died in 1884 of typhoid fever at the age of fifteen.

survey in the spring of 1861. Huntington, Crocker, Hopkins, and Stanford were encouraged by Judah's work. They soon agreed to form the Central Pacific Railroad. They elected Stanford as the company's first president. He would become the most famous of the "Big Four." He would soon be elected governor of California. He later became the Southern Pacific Company's third president. (The Southern Pacific Company was originally the Central Pacific Railroad.)

Stanford was expected to raise money for the railroad. He received millions in support from the state of California. At first, the only purpose of the Central Pacific was to construct a railroad from Sacramento to the Nevada border. This line would connect with the gold-mining camps. But this railway would soon receive another mandate.

As for his partners, they had their roles to play as well. Huntington, the Central Pacific's vice president, moved to New York City. There he convinced investors to buy stock and purchased equipment and materials needed for western rail construction. He delivered these by ship around South America to San Francisco. Investors did not flock in support of the railroad, however.

Collis P. Huntington (pictured) had owned a hardware business with Mark Hopkins before the two became interested in railroads.

The Civil War was on, and the eastern economy was shaky. It was experiencing inflation, an economic situation that drives prices up. At the same time, the value of the nation's paper money was dropping. The federal government began printing paper money during the war to help pay for its cost. Americans were not accustomed to a national paper currency and did not like to use it. Instead, they preferred using gold and silver coins.

Charles Crocker formed his own construction contracting business, the Charles Crocker Contract and Finance Company. His company, naturally, received the contract for building the first section of railroad from Sacramento to Roseville, a small settlement less than twenty miles away. Crocker hired the construction companies responsible for the actual railroad building.

Hopkins was selected as the treasurer for the Central Pacific Railroad. As for Judah, he remained on the scene and was also an investor in the company. He worried about the financial arrangements the Big Four had created. He thought they might only be interested in lining their own pockets with profits. But he would not live long enough to have a long-term impact on the workings of the Central Pacific. He died in November 1863, from yellow fever, which he had contracted in Panama during one of his many trips back east. On the day he died, construction on the railroad at Sacramento began.[6]

With the passage of the 1862 Pacific Railroad Act, the goals of the Central Pacific changed. They became national rather than regional. The act created the

Before getting involved with the first transcontinental railroad, General Samuel R. Curtis had led the Union Army to victory at the Battle of Pea Ridge in the Civil War.

Union Pacific Railroad and Telegraph Company. Its business framework was different from the Central Pacific. It included 163 commissioners. These leaders then appointed one of their own, Samuel R. Curtis, as their temporary chairman. Immediately, the corporation began selling stock. Investors who purchased shares of such stock became part owners in the company. The money they paid to buy the stock was used by the company. It paid for workers, equipment, and materials needed to build the railroad line. When the commissioners met later in September 1862, they elected William B. Ogden as president. They also chose Peter Dey to be the railroad's chief construction engineer. Ogden was known as a railroad promoter. (He had also served during the 1840s as Chicago's first elected mayor.) But, for a year, no progress in construction was made on the Union Pacific line.

The Beginning of the Great Road

Railroad officials held an official groundbreaking ceremony on December 2, 1863. Construction would begin in Nebraska. However, there was no rail bridge yet across the Missouri River from Council Bluffs to Omaha. So, construction did not begin immediately. In fact, no progress was made through the winter of 1863–1864. Workers were few. Equipment was in short supply. Progress was slow. The route still had to be graded. It had to be leveled out by removing earth from one part of the route and adding to another. The workers had to build a level earthen platform ready for track standing about two feet above the normal lay of the land. Drainage ditches were excavated along both sides of the grade.

Construction on the Union Pacific Railroad

Grading began that March. Some of the first graders included local American Indian women, members of the Omaha tribe.[1] More workers were soon hired, and some progress was made. Early on, workers built a sawmill to cut wooden rail ties from local cottonwood trees. A seventy-ton "shop locomotive" that had no wheels but remained stationary was delivered. Only in early July did the first regular locomotive arrive, the Union Pacific's (UP's) *General Sherman*. By then, fifty miles of the rail route had been graded and was ready for track. On July 10, the first iron rails were laid across the wooden cross ties. They were fitted into special metal flanges called fishplates.

After more than six months, the first ties were being laid. Far down the UP's proposed rail line, three surveying teams were still deciding on the exact route each leg of the company's rail line would follow. One team was in central Nebraska determining the line to the Wyoming Black Hills. A second was looking for the best rail crossing site through the Black Hills. Meanwhile, the third crew was laying the route between the western edge of the Black Hills and the Great Salt Lake. Workers, then, were scattered up and down the UP line for hundreds of miles.

But these early efforts were small baby steps for the Union Pacific. Various problems plagued the railroad's advance. There was a lack of available timber for rail ties. Such ties needed to be cut from hardwood trees, such as oak, maple, ash, or beech. But the Nebraska plains was home to few trees. Local trees were mostly soft cottonwoods that grew along river bottoms. The cottonwoods were unsuitable for long-term use as rail ties. The wood was not hard enough to support railroad traffic. Cottonwood was too soft to hold the spikes the workmen drove into the ties to hold the rails in place.

A special chemical process was introduced to help with the cottonwood problem. The process was called "Burnettizing," after an English chemist, William Burnett. It was done by a special machine that could hold 250 rail ties. A steam-powered pump pulled air from the drum holding the ties. Then, they were soaked for three hours in a zinc chloride solution. The process made the cottonwoods heavier and filled them with a metallic

Laborers work to Burnettize railroad ties in a rail yard in Omaha, Nebraska.

compound. Over the long haul, however, Burnettizing did not work as well as using hardwoods. Several years after the first transcontinental rail line was laid, these zinc-soaked ties had to be removed and replaced with new ties.

Progress along the Union Pacific end of the transcontinental line barely crept along through 1864. By year's end, not a single mile of track had been put into place by the UP. The graders had managed to grade about twenty miles of roadbed.[2] Construction was, in part, held back by a route change outside of Omaha. Late in the year, Thomas Durant shut down all grading work. Soon, a friend of his arrived at the work site. Colonel Silas Seymour changed the route that Dey had already laid out. Seymour's new survey added nine more miles to the UP route. The purpose was clear to Dey. Durant wanted to add mileage to the UP line because the government paid for every mile of track constructed.

By adding nine more miles, the company would receive nearly $144,000 more in bonds and more than 115,000 acres of government-owned land. Such tricks took place during the first Transcontinental Railroad's construction. Unfortunately, the delay in construction slowed the UP's advance even more. Workers lost months of valuable building time. As late as the spring of 1865, when the Civil War ended, the UP had not managed to lay any track outside the city limits of Omaha. Eventually, Dey would tire of the schemes and frauds. He quit his job in December 1864, leaving the UP with no chief construction engineer.[3]

Enter Grenville Dodge

When Dey resigned, he was eventually replaced by one of the men who would become one of the most important employees of the Union Pacific. Grenville Dodge was an expert railroad engineer and old friend of Durant's. The two men had surveyed railroads together back in the 1850s. General Dodge had served in the Civil War. Through much of the war, he built military railroads for the Union Army.

While he was working as engineer of the Union Pacific Railroad, Major General Grenville Dodge founded the town of Cheyenne, Wyoming. This photo was taken during the Civil War.

The UP wanted to hire Dodge to take Dey's place. But, before he was hired, President Lincoln sent him out West in January 1865. His task was to subdue Great Plains Indians who were attacking settlements in Kansas and Colorado, as well as along the UP route. Dodge moved his headquarters out to Fort Leavenworth, Kansas. His orders from General Ulysses Grant were "to remove all trespassers [Indians] on land of the Union Pacific Railroad."[4] Dodge had accepted the offer from

Durant to take the chief engineer's job. But it would have to wait until his campaign against the American Indians was finished.

Problems for the UP

One of the major problems plaguing the UP early on was a lack of workers. Much of this problem was solved with the end of the Civil War in April 1865. Soon after the bloody American conflict was over, thousands of men came west in search of work. Many were veterans and immigrants, especially Irish and German workers. There were Mexicans, Englishmen, ex-Confederates, and African Americans who had once been slaves. Railroad work represented better pay for many laborers.[5]

Another construction problem was a shortage of supplies and equipment. Construction began east of Omaha before a bridge was built over the Missouri River. Construction materials and equipment had to be delivered by steamboat or ferry across the river. Much of it was brought up the Missouri from St. Joseph, Missouri, more than 175 miles downriver.[6]

Another problem the UP faced through 1864 was a lack of money. Under the original 1862 Railroad Act, Congress had required the completion of forty miles of western track before either railroad could receive its first government bonds. It was hard to convince investors to spend their money on western railroad construction. Money issues became so severe that President Lincoln even stepped in. He asked Congressman Oakes

Ames to use his political power and personal wealth to jump-start investment in the UP. Ames and his brother, Oliver, had made millions in a family business that sold shovels and other tools. The Ames brothers soon bought $1 million in Credit Mobilier stock, and Oakes personally loaned six hundred thousand dollars to the UP. Once the Ameses invested in the UP end of the transcontinental railroad, other investors suddenly appeared.[7]

The war was finally over, and workers began appearing by the thousands. By the summer of 1865, work was slowly advancing on the Union Pacific line. By late September, eleven miles of track had been completed. A month later, nine more miles were finished. The UP was beginning to pick up speed. That fall, UP workers were laying a half mile of track daily. That same September, General Dodge was still engaged in Indian campaigns, then along the Powder River in Wyoming.

The UP's tracklaying finally began to pick up speed. Thomas Durant decided it was time to celebrate the company's progress. That November, he invited General William Tecumseh Sherman, one of the Union heroes of the Civil War, to come to Nebraska for an official ceremony. Sherman showed up and took a ride on the line:

> To please Sherman they painted the general's name in gilt letters on Union Pacific Locomotive No. 1. As no passenger cars had yet been brought up the Missouri, they attached to the Iron Horse a platform car covered with upended nail kegs to

General William Tecumseh Sherman won a series of key battles to help bring about the end of the Civil War. After the war, Sherman advised on the transcontinental railroad.

which boards were fastened for seats. Sherman, Durant, Train, and the dozen or so other men in the party wrapped themselves in buffalo robes and rode the fifteen miles to end of track at Sailing's Grove, where they picknicked on roast duck and champagne.[8]

Sherman later gave a speech. Even though Durant and the other UP officials had put their best foot forward that day, Sherman left without having been impressed. Sherman later noted: "I might live to see the day, but can scarcely expect it at my age, when the two oceans will be connected by a complete Pacific railroad."[9] By year's end, the UP had finished laying its first forty miles of track.

The Central Pacific and the Sierra Nevadas

Slowly, the Union Pacific inched its way west. Back in California, progress on the Central Pacific was facing its own problems. The Central Pacific (CP), like the UP, also faced shortages of building materials and equipment. The railroad also had an inadequate crew of workers. When white workers failed to appear in adequate numbers, the CP faced difficult choices. In the spring of 1865, only eight hundred men were working for the CP.[10] The CP needed four thousand more. This labor shortage spurred the Central Pacific's Charles Crocker to suggest the hiring of Chinese laborers. His suggestion paid off immediately. By the spring of 1866, more than eight thousand Chinese were laboring for the CP.[11] The total number of Chinese laborers working for the CP would finally top out at twelve thousand.[12]

By June 1865, CP railroad construction was nearing the base of the Sierra Nevadas. That month, it reached Clipper Gap. Behind it lay forty-three miles of completed track stretching westward to Sacramento. The mountains lay fifty-eight miles in front, including Donner Pass. The tracks the CP laid through this natural barrier rose five thousand feet above the foothills of the Sierra Nevadas. Some engineering experts did not believe the line could be constructed. Chinese workers would prove them wrong.

Chinese workers toiled hard under their Irish gang bosses, who were usually hard talking and rough around the edges. The Chinese removed tons of rock and debris, set explosive charges, and did most of the dangerous, mountainous work. They managed to cut ledges for track along sheer cliffs and blast tunnels out of solid granite. Their work ethic was never questioned and often praised:

> They are ready to begin work the moment they
> hear the signal, and labor steadily and honestly on
> till admonished that the working hours are ended.

> They have no story-telling; they have no sentinel set to watch while his companions enjoy their pipes, and to pass the word when the "boss" comes in sight. Not having acquired a taste for whiskey, they have few fights, and no "blue Mondays."[13]

The Chinese workers became the driving force of the Central Pacific. Perhaps no workers on the Transcontinental Railroad risked their lives in more ways. They died under rock slides and by accidental explosions. They fell off cliff sides. Some were buried under avalanches of snow and froze to death.

New Drivers on the UP

Back on the UP end of the rail line, Durant remained disappointed. General Dodge remained in military service from the fall of 1865 through the spring of 1866. Progress crept along on the UP end of the transcontinental line. The year 1865 saw little advancement of the line. There was a new pressure on Durant as well. Congress had passed a new railroad bill, the 1864 Pacific Railroad Act. The new act provided needed monies sooner to the railroads. The act reduced from forty to twenty the number of miles of completed track to be finished before government bonds would be paid to the railroads. The act also doubled the government's land grants to ten sections per mile, a total of 12,800 acres. In a change from the 1862 Pacific Railroad Act, the railroads were deeded mineral rights to these lands. Concerned about a lack of progress on the western line, the congressional act required the Union Pacific to complete at least one hundred miles of track by June 27, 1866. The odds of completing that many miles looked slim for the UP. By the end of 1865, only forty miles had been laid.[14]

Construction on the UP needed a serious shot in the arm. Thomas Durant found what he needed when

One observer said the Casement brothers looked like "twelve-year-old boys, but requiring larger hats."

he hired a pair of brothers, John "Jack" Stephen and Dan Casement. They were both veterans of the Civil War. (John had served as a brigadier general.) The Casements had experience as railroad engineers in Ohio. Both were short: John stood five feet four inches tall, while brother Dan stood "five feet nothing."[15] One observer said the Casement brothers looked like "twelve-year-old boys, but requiring larger hats."[16] But they were stocky, strong and powerful men. One story described how Dan Casement "once . . . lifted a 30 foot rail off the ground without any trouble. It weighed about 600 pounds."[17] The Casements signed a contract with Thomas Durant to be paid $750 for each mile of track they laid. Since the Casements worked under personal contract, they were their own bosses. Soon, the brothers were the movers and shakers who would drive construction to new heights.[18]

Then, by late April 1866, General Dodge was ready
to leave his Army command. He prepared to begin his
duties with the Union Pacific. He received a leave of
absence from General Sherman on May 1. In his letter
to Dodge, Sherman saw the future of the Union Pacific
and the completion of the Transcontinental Railroad.
To Sherman, it all rested squarely on Dodge's shoul-
ders: "I consent to your going to begin what, I trust, will
be the real beginning of the great road."[19] Once Dodge
arrived in Omaha, he began his work as chief engineer
with fervor. He began running the UP like a civilian
army. Many of those who worked directly under him
were Civil War veterans. Military discipline seemed just
the thing to whip the UP and its workers into shape.
There were still American Indians along the UP route,
including the Sioux and Cheyenne. Dodge vowed to
command a fierce defense if they ever attacked. When
Dodge began his duties that spring, he was paid a salary
of ten thousand dollars, a considerable sum at that time.

Due to Dodge and the Casements, progress on the
Union Pacific's end of the transcontinental line sped up
significantly by 1866. Only about forty miles of track
were completed during the first two years of construction. But the Casements oversaw the construction of
266 miles of track in 1866 alone. The key was organiza-
tion and good planning.

An Organized Effort

Every step of construction had to be well planned.
Sometimes working as far as three hundred miles to

the west of rail construction, the UP surveyors staked out the specific sites where track should be laid. Roadbed crews would follow behind them. They used horse and mule teams to pull scrapping machines to level out the route. The teams of railroad "roustabouts" filled dump carts, using shovels provided by the Ames Old Colony Shovel Company.

Following the graders were the bridge builders, who generally worked twenty miles ahead of the site where track was being laid. These structures were typically trestles that crossed rivers or low valley spots where the grade of the track would be too steep to follow the curve of the land. Since timber was in short supply across most of the Great Plains, the UP came to rely on logs and bridge timbers cut in Minnesota.

These timbers were floated down the Mississippi and up the Missouri to Omaha. There, they were cut to a specific size to fit a planned trestle. Mule teams delivered them to the construction site. While the trestle builders worked, additional crews delivered hundreds of wooden ties for later use. Most of the ties were Burnettized cottonwoods. Often every fifth tie was a hardwood, either cedar or oak, which was also shipped in from distant forests.[20]

Bosses on the UP had to coordinate the surveying,

Credit Mobilier

By 1866, Congressman Oakes Ames and his brother, Oliver, had taken control of the Union Pacific by investing in stock in Credit Mobilier, a fake company they created. Although the company was a "dummy" corporation, its "owners" were allowed to sell construction contracts. This resulted in huge profits for the owners.

This trestle was built by the Central Pacific Railroad.

grading, bridging, and the delivery of material at each construction site. Then, a tracklaying train arrived. Such work trains included several flatcars carrying workmen's tools, as well as a mobile blacksmith shop. To house the workers, a typical work train included three immense sleeping cars measuring eighty-five feet long. These cars were filled with rows of bunks.

They were twice the size of a regular boxcar. Up to three hundred or four hundred men could sleep in these cars.[21] If the work crew numbered more than that, men slept in tents. Some even hung hammocks underneath the railcars. These trains also included a dining car where 125 men could eat at the same time, seated at one long table. The tin plates were nailed to the table. After each use, dish swabbers wiped them out between meals. Another car housed the kitchen, a storeroom, and the engineer's office. Outside this rail car were animal carcasses hanging from hooks. This provided fresh meat for the workers. These animals were usually killed by hunters who contracted with the railroad. These special trains were not pulled, but pushed from behind by a locomotive.

Each morning, the work crews completed a new section of track, then moved farther down the line. As they worked, they filled the prairie with a racket of steel striking steel. Crews of six men worked together. They began their morning loading sixteen rails into small wagons, plus the number of spikes, bolts, and fishplates needed to secure their rails in place. As they worked laying track, the rails were removed in pairs, with five men carrying one rail. Each rail weighed five hundred or six hundred pounds. A notched piece of wood was used to separate each pair of rails at the appropriate distance from one another. The standard rail gauge in use at that time was four feet eight and a-half inches. This marked the distance from one rail wheel to its opposite.[22]

Once a pair of rails was in place, spike men began driving their spikes into the ties to secure the rails. On average, a skilled spike man could drive a spike in place with three blows from his hammer. An expert team of rail layers could put a pair of rails in place in a minute. This process would have to be repeated four hundred times per mile. That is how many pairs of rails it took to cover that distance. When in full swing, the noise created by rail work crews was metallic and constant. As one newspaper reporter wrote: "A grand Anvil Chorus [is] playing across the plains . . . 21 million [strokes and] this great work of modern America is complete."[23]

In time, the Casements organized one hundred teams, comprised of approximately one thousand men. They were paid according to their skills. Regular, unskilled workers were paid $2.50 per day. Spikers were paid three dollars. Ironworkers received four dollars for their skills. As each team completed its section of track, the entire workforce moved farther down the line, ready to lay new track. Slowly, but steadily, the rails of the Union Pacific snaked their way across Nebraska.[24]

The workers suffered many injuries and accidents, as well as deadly diseases. Indian raids across Nebraska and Wyoming

"Hell-on-Wheels"

Not everyone in the worker camps was employed by the railroad. On the edge of many camps were followers who included gamblers, saloon keepers, con men, and prostitutes. The rail workers often spent their hard-earned pay on the services of these people. Life in these camps was sometimes dangerous, even deadly. Violence was common. Critics referred to these camps as "Hell-on-Wheels."

On August 4, 1867, Cheyenne Indians attacked a working party on the Union Pacific Railroad. The battle was sketched by T. R. Davis for the September 7, 1867 issue of *Harper's Weekly*.

occurred repeatedly. Several workers were killed. Indian warriors roamed in large numbers. They often pulled out the stakes surveyors used to mark their route. On May 25, 1867, five workmen were killed by Indians near Overton, Nebraska. One of the most famous American Indian raids took place on August 6, 1867. Near Plum Creek, Nebraska (230 miles west of Omaha), Indians attacked a handcar carrying five rail workers. One of the workers was scalped but lived by pretending to be dead. The Cheyenne warriors then tore up several rails, which later caused a five-car train to wreck. The engineer and his fireman were both killed. Eventually, Dodge required all UP workers to be armed.[25]

Transcontinental Railroad Route

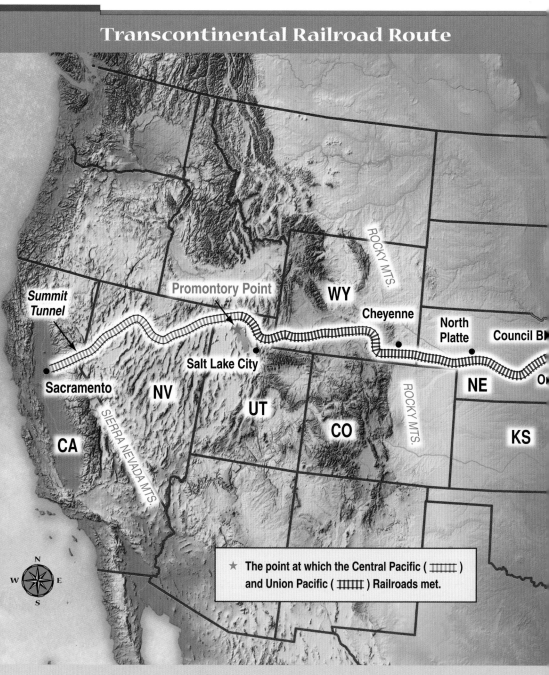

The route of the transcontinental railroad crossed the plains and the mountains of the United States.

The End of the Line

By the spring of 1867, the Summit Tunnel was completed by the Central Pacific's (CP's) Chinese workmen. Work crews had suffered forty-four snowstorms and blizzards. With the threat of snows across the highlands of the Sierra Nevadas, CP workers built thirty-seven miles of snowsheds over their tracks. These were large, wooden-framed tunnels, designed to keep snows off the rails. Some of the sheds were reinforced with brick and mortar.[1]

That spring, progress continued as the CP continued carving through the mountains. By June, work crews reached Donner Summit. A short-lived Chinese worker strike stopped construction for a while. But Crocker refused to pay them better wages. He forced them back to work by cutting off their supply of special foods.[2] Before year's end, the CP managed to build an additional forty-seven miles of track. Workers finally cut through to the east side of the Sierras into the Truckee Valley.

The flatlands of Nevada were in front of them, and the great mountain barrier was finally behind them. Crocker pushed his workers to pick up their speed. He

In the Sierra Nevada mountains in California, workers built snow sheds to protect trains and tracks from heavy snowfall.

hoped his men could hit a pace of one mile of track laid per day by 1868. He would not be disappointed. The goal of the CP had become to beat the Union Pacific (UP) to the Mormon settlements around the Great Salt Lake. The Mormons were a religious sect that had migrated out to Utah during the late 1840s and early 1850s. The railroad that reached the Mormons first would have access to the lucrative market provided by the members of the Church of Jesus Christ of Latter-Day Saints. But there were six hundred miles between the California-Nevada border (the location of the Truckee Valley) and the valley of the Great Salt Lake.

CP and UP survey crews scrambled to develop a

route to the Mormon settlements. But they soon discovered that a rail line north of the Salt Lake would be better than one skirting around the south side of the lake near Salt Lake City, the largest Mormon settlement. General Dodge wrote about the conclusions of his UP survey team:

> The northern route was shorter by 76 miles, had less ascent and descent, less elevation to overcome, less curvature, and the total cost was $2.5 million less. There was more running water, more lumber, and better land for agriculture and grazing.[3]

Both the CP and UP decided to bypass Salt Lake City by thirty miles. Instead, they would run the railroad through Ogden, north of the lake. As for the Mormon leader and elder Brigham Young, he was furious. He protested to the federal government. He even preached against Grenville Dodge from the pulpit. He offered special incentives to the railroads, including free food and supplies for their work crews. But neither railroad gave in to Young's demands.[4] But after the transcontinental line was completed, a branch line to Salt Lake City was built.

Picking Up Speed

The year 1868 was the last full year of construction for the UP and CP before they met on a barren upland plain in Utah. January 8 marked the fifth-year anniversary of the CP's groundbreaking ceremony in Sacramento. The CP had built just 146 miles of track during those years, less than thirty miles annually. Cutting through the Sierra Nevadas had been slow and costly. Perhaps as many as five hundred workers had died, maybe as many as one thousand. As for the UP, they had constructed 520 miles of track during those same five years.[5]

By May, the Central Pacific reached Lake Crossing, west of the California-Nevada border. The CP built a depot station at the lake and renamed the site after a favorite Civil War commander of some of the CP officials, General Jesse Reno. Today, the site is Reno, Nevada.

The rail workers continued their advance, following the Truckee River, then heading northeast past the source of the Humboldt River. Following the Humboldt, tracks were laid to a desert town, Winemucca, by June 1868. Ahead were the flats of Nevada. Soon, construction crews were plagued by a new problem—water. The region was desert dotted by few trees and sagebrush. Springs were few, and often the water was full of alkali and too bitter to drink. Water had to be piped in from springs workers found north of the rail line. As for construction, it was easy work. The soil was loose and easy to level out. Never had the CP work crews laid so much track so quickly.[6] Soon, they were averaging a

New Towns

As the Union Pacific moved west, rail depots were constructed. Later, permanent towns sprang up. Today, these include such towns as North Platte, Nebraska; Julesburg, Colorado; and Cheyenne, Wyoming.

mile of construction a day, just as Crocker had hoped. By November 1868, the CP reached Palisade Canyon in eastern Nevada. The Central Pacific constructed 360 miles of track in 1868. The Union Pacific outstripped them with 425.[7] That December, CP survey crews had mapped out a route north of the Great Salt Lake, past Promontory, Utah, to Echo Canyon. Nearby were rival UP survey crews.[8]

The Railroads Approach One Another

By the spring of 1869, both the CP and the UP were laying track at an amazing pace. The Union Pacific work crews hit their greatest strides. They sometimes laid as much as four miles of track in a single day. On one day, UP trackmen laid eight-and-a-half miles of track. By January 9, 1869, work crews of the UP laid their one-thousandth mile out of Omaha. They crossed the border into Utah by late December 1868. Once in Utah, the Union Pacific had to dig their first tunnels, having reached the Wasatch Range. They would carve out four tunnels in all. (Through the Sierra Nevadas, the CP had blasted out fifteen tunnels.) The longest UP tunnel was at Echo Canyon, measuring nearly eight hundred feet long. But tunnel work slowed the UP's progress. So, workers laid a line around Echo Summit, Utah, so track work could continue. As for the tunnel at Echo Canyon, it would be finished later.[9] At Weber Canyon, another two tunnels were excavated. A giant trestle was built across a local gorge. The "Big Trestle" was enormous, measuring four hundred feet long and eighty-five feet in height.[10]

Soon, the two railroads were laying track near one another. But there was no established meeting point for the two rail lines. Since every mile of track meant more money in bonds, the CP and UP crews just kept laying track until they finally passed one another. CP work crews even labored at night by lamplight. Across the Utah landscape, the two railroads continued to build, each laying track over the same ground for a distance of two hundred miles. Sometimes, UP and CP work crews were so close to one another that one crew's explosive charges scattered rock and debris on their rival work crews.[11] By January, a federally appointed commission chose Promontory Summit, fifty-six miles west of Ogden, Utah, as the official meeting point for the UP and CP lines. Work continued over the next few months as the lines approached one another. Late in April, a CP work crew of Chinese and Irish laborers laid ten miles of track in twelve hours, establishing a new record.[12]

"Done"

The date was set for the official connecting of the two rail lines: May 8. The president of the CP, Leland Stanford, came out to Utah on a special train filled with railroad officials, government dignitaries, and reporters. The group traveled in an elaborate passenger car called the Presidential Special. From the East, UP officials Grenville Dodge and Dr. Thomas Durant took their own train, traveling in a special car dubbed the Lincoln Car. Along the way, they faced bad weather, including torrential rains that washed out some rail grades and several bridges and made crossing one of the UP trestles quite dangerous. Repairs were made, directed by Dodge and Durant personally. At one point, they nearly had to abandon the Lincoln Car and continue on horseback. But after waiting an

They all came out to witness the historic linking of the United States by rail.

extra day, the weather turned and they were able to continue on to Promontory. Their delay postponed the planned ceremonies by two days.

May 10, 1869, was a bright and sunny day. The desert lands near Promontory played host to six hundred people, including many locals. They all came out to witness the historic linking of the United States by rail. In addition to Stanford, Dodge, and Durant, the Casement brothers were also present. Four companies of the U.S. Army's 21st Infantry Regiment were on hand, lined up in double columns along the rail tracks.[13]

At 12:27 P.M., a minister from Massachusetts and a Mormon elder each delivered a prayer. Four special spikes were presented, including two made of gold, one of silver, and another of silver, gold, and iron. On one of the golden spikes was an inscription: "May God continue the unity of our Country as this Railroad unites the two great Oceans of the world."[14] They were dropped, not hammered, into prepared holes. Leland

The locomotive Jupiter was used during the meeting of the Central Pacific and Union Pacific railroads on May 10, 1869, in Promontory Point, Utah.

Stanford, the highest-ranking official in attendance, was given the honor of striking a hammer blow to a fifth iron spike into a rail tie. Durant would swing the second blow. This spike was attached to telegraph wires. Once the spike was struck, it would complete an electrical circuit and signal to all Americans up and down the telegraph line that the transcontinental line was completed. Hundreds of witnesses watched the two railroad officials take their turn at the hammer. Both Stanford and Durant missed the spike completely. But a telegraph operator watching nearby tapped out the word that went out to telegraph stations from the

Pacific Coast to the Atlantic: "Done."[15] The crowd cheered. The time in Utah was 12:47 P.M.

On the tracks, two locomotives faced one another—the Central Pacific's wood-burning engine, *Jupiter*, and the UP's *Engine No. 119*, a coal burner. A photographer prepared to take a commemorative photo of the historic event. The two engines were eased toward one another. Rail workmen climbed onto each engine. With the two engines nearly cowcatcher to cowcatcher, the engineers on each locomotive emerged and scrambled onto the boiler fronts. Each handed the other a bottle of champagne. Grenville Dodge stood in the foreground

At a special ceremony, workers, engineers, and supervisors of the Central Pacific and Union Pacific Railroads celebrated the completion of the transcontinental railroad at Promontory Point, Utah, on May 10, 1869.

The *119* was one of the locomotives that was used to celebrate the meeting of the rails at Promontory Point. Today, it can be seen at the Golden Spike National Historical Site in Promontory, Point, Utah.

shaking hands with the CP's chief engineer, Samuel Montague. The photo was taken, etching an image that would be reproduced in countless history books. The railroads were linked together by a thin ribbon of steel and iron. And with it, the United States, its East and its West, became united as never before.

Additional Railroads West

The completion of the Transcontinental Railroad in the spring of 1869 was just the beginning for railroad expansion across the West. Within a generation, four more transcontinental lines had reached the West

Coast: the Southern Pacific and the Northern Pacific (both completed in 1883); the Atchison, Topeka and Santa Fe (1885); and the Great Northern (1893). During the 1880s alone, forty thousand miles of track were built.[16] Feeder lines were built, connecting one transcontinental line to another, creating a spidery pattern of railroad expansion. In 1852, only five miles of rail line—a short line called the Pacific Railroad of Missouri—ran west of the Mississippi. By 1890, the lands of the Trans-Mississippi River region were crisscrossed by seventy-two thousand miles of rail.[17] As for the first two western railroads, the Union Pacific and Central Pacific, their futures went in different

The Union Pacific still operates trains throughout the country. This train climbs Cajon Pass in California.

directions. The Union Pacific continued as a separate rail company and still exists today. But, by 1885, the CP became part of the Southern Pacific Railroad, which also continued into modern times.

The railroads gave support to the development of the Far West and Great Plains regions. Their iron rails delivered trains to mining camps, army posts, farms, and ranches, thus speeding up the settlement of these western frontiers. With the arrival of the railroads across the West, the landscape was soon filled with millions of emigrants and immigrants. Railroad agents recruited easterners to come out west. They even traveled to Europe, where they convinced an endless stream of Germans, Swedes, Danes, Norwegians, Finns, Irish, and others to sell out, pack up, and move to the American West.[18]

Most—Americans and Europeans alike—built farms. They had been encouraged to move onto the Great Plains by federal laws, especially the Homestead Act of 1862, which granted 160 acres of free land to anyone who was willing to give western farming a try. The act made such land available even to foreign immigrants who were not yet American citizens (the law only denied land to former Confederates). Tens of thousands of homesteads were established. In 1871 alone, more than twenty thousand land claims were filed under the Homestead Act involving 2.5 million acres. While many such farmers failed, the move onto the Great Plains continued through the rest of the nineteenth century.[19]

With the advancement of the railroads, the West became a home to countless millions of new arrivals. The frontier ceased to exist and, in fact, was gone by the time the Great Northern opened its operations

American civilization crossed the Great Plains on rails.

in the early 1890s. American civilization crossed the Great Plains on rails. This march of humanity and its impact on the frontier was predicted even before the first transcontinental railroad was completed. Even as the dream of such a rail line was being formed in the minds of men such as Asa Whitney, Theodore Judah, Stephen Douglas, and Leland Stanford, there were those who saw even greater visions of the future. These visions were seen by men like William Gilpin, who described the impact the transcontinental line would bring to the United States:

> In the ripeness of time the hope of humanity is realized ... [This] continental railway ... will bind the two seaboards to this one continental union like ears to the human head; [to plant] the foundation of the Union so broad and deep ... that no possible force or [plan] can shake its permanence.[20]

Gilpin's remarks reinforced the belief of many Americans: A railroad that linked the various parts of the country would make the United States a much stronger nation for years to come.

1780s One hundred thousand Anglo-Americans make the Trans-Appalachian region their home.

1785 Land Ordinance of 1785 calls for survey and land distribution throughout the territory of the Old Northwest. The new law creates townships with sections of 640 acres each.

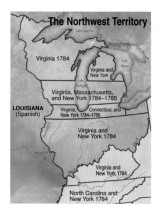

1795 One hundred fifty thousand Anglo-Americans live west of the linear ridges of the Appalachians.

1802 Congress passes an act calling for the construction of a federally funded highway, the National Road, that will extend from Maryland through the Old Northwest.

1803 The United States purchases the vast territory of Louisiana from the French government.

1804–1806 Lewis and Clark explore the Louisiana Purchase Territory.

1810 According to the census, more than one million Americans are living in the Trans-Appalachian region.

1820–1845 Approximately eighty thousand Americans push their way into the Southwest, including Texas.

1825 Opening of New York's Erie Canal encourages migration of pioneers into the Old Northwest and even farther west.

1828 America's first railroad, the Baltimore & Ohio, is opened for business.

1845 United States annexes the Republic of Texas as a new state. That same year, New York City merchant Asa Whitney proposes to Congress the building of the first transcontinental railroad.

1849 Gold seekers flock to California during the Gold Rush. The following year, the territory is added to the United States as a new state.

1840s–1860s Hundreds of thousands of Americans travel west along the Oregon and California trails.

1853 Passing the Pacific Railroad Survey Act, Congress sets aside $150,000 for surveying possible routes for a transcontinental railroad.

1854 Congress passes the Kansas-Nebraska Act, opening up the region for construction of a northern route for the Transcontinental Railroad.

1858 The Butterfield Overland Express, the first

stagecoach line to span the Great Plains to California, opens for business.

1861 California investors create the Central Pacific Railroad, electing Leland Stanford as the railroad's first president.

1862 President Lincoln signs the Pacific Railroad Act, clearing the way for construction of America's first railroad across the West. The act creates the Union Pacific Railroad Company. That same year, the Homestead Act is passed, offering free western land on the Great Plains.

1863 Official groundbreaking ceremony in Nebraska marks the beginning of construction on the eastern end of the Transcontinental Railroad.

1864 Little progress is made by either the CP or UP in construction of the great western railroad.

1865 With the Civil War over that spring, the UP gains the workers it needs to speed up tracklaying across Nebraska. That same year, the CP begins hiring Chinese laborers to work on railroad construction.

1867 Central Pacific work crews complete the "Summit Tunnel" in the Sierra Nevadas.

1868 During this last full year of railroad construction on the transcontinental line, the CP completes 360 miles of track while the UP completes 425 miles.

May 10, 1869 The CP and UP link up near Promontory Point, Utah, completing America's first transcontinental rail line.

1866–1885 Cowboys drive Texas Longhorn cattle north to railhead in Kansas by the "Long Drive."

1883 Two additional transcontinental railroads are completed: the Southern Pacific and the Northern Pacific.

1885 A fourth western line is completed, the Atchison, Topeka and Santa Fe.

1890 The land of the Trans-Mississippi West is spanned by seventy-two thousand miles of railroad tracks.

1893 A fifth western line, the Great Northern Railroad is completed.

Chapter One   "Without Them It Would Be Impossible"

1. Robert West Howard, *The Great Iron Trail: The Story of the First Trans-Continental Railroad* (New York: G. P. Putnam's Sons, 1962), p. 227.

2. Stephen E. Ambrose, *Nothing Like It in the World: The Men Who Built the Transcontinental Railroad, 1863–1869* (New York: Simon & Schuster, 2000), p. 38.

3. Ibid., p. 150.

4. Howard, p. 225.

5. Ibid.

6. Keith Wheeler, *The Railroaders* (New York: Time-Life Books, 1973), p. 92.

7. Howard, p. 226.

8. Geoffrey C. Ward, *The West: An Illustrated History* (Boston: Little, Brown and Company, 1996), p. 244.

9. Ambrose, p. 154.

10. Howard, p. 229.

11. Ward, p. 247.

12. Howard, p. 231.

13. Wheeler, p. 105.

14. Ward, p. 246.

15. Ambrose, p. 236.

16. Wheeler, p. 105.

17. Ward, p. 247.

18. Ibid.

19. Ibid., p. 250.

Chapter Two   Between the Known and the Unknown

1. Malcolm Rohrbough, *The Trans-Appalachian Frontier: People, Societies, and Institutions 1775–1850* (New York: Oxford University Press, 1978), p. 25.

2. Ibid., p. 71.

3. Bartlett, p. 144.

4. Ibid., p. 319.

5. Bartlett, pp. 319–320.

6. Ibid., p. 321.

7. Ibid., p. 322.

8. Robert West Howard, *The Great Iron Trail: The Story of the First Trans-Continental Railroad* (New York: G. P. Putnam's Sons, 1962), p. 19.

9. Oliver Jensen, *The American Heritage History of Railroads in America* (New York: Bonanza Books, 1975), p. 48.

10. Ibid.

11. Keith Wheeler, *The Railroaders* (New York: Time-Life Books, 1973), p. 40.

12. Bartlett, p. 325.

13. Ibid., p. 327.

14. Ibid., p. 325.

15. Ibid., p. 188.

Chapter Three   Into the West

1. Keith Wheeler, *The Railroaders* (New York: Time-Life Books, 1973), p. 308.

2. David Wishart, *The Fur Trade of the American West, 1807–1840* (Lincoln: University of Nebraska Press, 1979), p. 29.

3. Lynn Perrigo, The *American Southwest: Its People and Cultures* (New York: Holt, Rinehart, and Winston, 1971), p. 105.

4. W. Eugene Hollon, *The Southwest: Old and New* (New York: Alfred A. Knopf, 1961), p. 106.

5. Tim McNeese and Michael S. Mountjoy, *History in the Making: Sources and Essays of America's Past* (New York: American Heritage, 1994), p. 265.

6. Henry Steele Commager, ed., *The West: An Illustrated History* (New York: Promontory Press, 1976), p. 48.

7. Lillian Schlissel, *Women's Diaries of the Westward Journey* (New York: Schocken Books, 1992), p. 24.

8. Ibid., p. 22.

Chapter Four   "God Preserve This Whole Country"

1. Robert West Howard, *The Great Iron Trail: The Story of the First Trans-Continental Railroad* (New York: G. P. Putnam's Sons, 1962), p. 42.

2. Lynn Perrigo, *The American Southwest: Its People and Cultures* (New York: Holt, Rinehart, and Winston, 1971), p. 179.

3. Ibid.

4. J. S. Holliday, *The World Rushed In: The California Gold Rush Experience, An Eyewitness Account of a Nation Heading West* (New York: Simon and Schuster, 1981), pp. 42–43.

5. Ibid., p. 300.

6. Ibid., p. 397.

7. Henry Steele Commager, ed., *The West: An Illustrated History* (New York: Promontory Press, 1976), p. 160.

8. Ibid., p. 161.

9. Ibid., p. 178.

10. Ibid.

Chapter Five   **Planning America's Railroad**

1. Don Russell, ed., *Trails of the Iron Horse* (Garden City, N.J.: Doubleday & Company, Inc., 1975), pp. 12–13.

2. Robert West Howard, *The Great Iron Trail: The Story of the First Trans-Continental Railroad* (New York: G. P. Putnam's Sons, 1962), p. 66.

3. Gillian Houghton, *The Transcontinental Railroad* (New York: Rosen Publishing Group, Inc., 2003), p. 16.

4. James E. Vance, Jr., *The North American Railroad: Its Origin, Evolution, and Geography* (Baltimore: Johns Hopkins University Press, 1995), p. 169.

5. Howard, p. 120.

6. Houghton, p. 27.

Chapter Six   The Beginning of the Great Road

1. David Haward Bain, *Empire Express: Building the First Transcontinental Railroad* (New York: Viking Penguin, 1999), p. 182.

2. Stephen E. Ambrose, *Nothing Like It in the World: The Men Who Built the Transcontinental Railroad, 1863–1869* (New York: Simon & Schuster, 2000), p. 99.

3. Ibid., pp. 98–99.

4. Ibid., p. 130.

5. Geoffrey C. Ward, *The West: An Illustrated History* (Boston: Little, Brown and Company, 1996), p. 222.

6. Ambrose, p. 133.

7. Keith Wheeler, *The Railroaders* (New York: Time-Life Books, 1973), p. 72.

8. Dee Brown, *Hear That Lonesome Whistle Blow: Railroads in the West* (New York: Holt, Rinehart, and Winston, 1977), p. 50.

9. Ibid., p. 61.

10. Bain, p. 208.

11. Ambrose, p. 198.

12. Bain, p. 209.

13. Wesley S. Griswold, *A Work of Giants* (New York: McGraw-Hill, 1962) p. 34.

14. Ambrose, p. 143.

15. Ibid., p. 170.

16. Wheeler, p. 92.

17. Ambrose, p. 171.

18. Wheeler, p. 92.

19. Ambrose, p. 171.

20. Wheeler, p. 99.

21. Ibid.

22. Ibid., p. 100.

23. Ibid., p. 91.

24. Ambrose, pp. 214, 222, 302 and Bain, pp. 387–388.

25. Ibid., pp. 70–71.

Chapter Seven The End of the Line

1. Robert West Howard, *The Great Iron Trail: The Story of the First Trans-Continental Railroad* (New York: G. P. Putnam's Sons, 1962), p. 272.

2. Stephen E. Ambrose, *Nothing Like It in the World: The Men Who Built the Transcontinental Railroad, 1863–1869* (New York: Simon & Schuster, 2000), p. 242.

3. Charles Edgar Ames, *Pioneering the Union Pacific: A Reappraisal of the Builders of the Railroad.* (New York: Meredith Corporation, 1969), pp. 22–23.

4. Ambrose, p. 286.

5. Howard, pp. 271–272.

6. Ambrose, pp. 302, 310–312.

7. Keith Wheeler, *The Railroaders* (New York: Time-Life Books, 1973), p. 112.

8. Bain, pp. 595–596 and Ambrose, p. 326.

9. Wheeler, p. 112.

10. Ambrose, p. 338.

11. Wheeler, pp. 112–113.

12. Ibid., p. 113.

13. Ambrose, p. 363.

14. Wheeler, p. 116.

15. Ambrose, p. 366.

16. Wheeler, p. 204.

17. Geoffrey C. Ward, *The West: An Illustrated History* (Boston: Little, Brown and Company, 1996), pp. 18, 91.

18. Bartlett, p. 332.

19. Henry Steele Commager, ed., *The West: An Illustrated History* (New York: Promontory Press, 1976), p. 220.

20. Ward, p. 228.

Burnettizing—Chemical process used to preserve railroad ties by removing the air from the ties and injecting them with a zinc chloride solution.

Conestoga wagon—Eighteenth century freight wagon developed by German immigrants living in the Conestoga Valley of Pennsylvania and known for its size and durability.

fish plate—Special metal pieces of metal attached to wooden railroad ties in which iron rails were secured.

flatboat—Homemade river craft that was constructed out of plank lumber and featured a flat bottom.

frontier—Region between area where Americans had set up towns and the farthest part of new land where settlers were building a new settlement.

Manifest Destiny—Belief concerning the West used by America pioneers to justify their seizure of the region from other peoples. The claim said that God intended Americans to occupy the land over all other peoples.

National Road—This east-to-west road was constructed by the federal government across Maryland, Pennsylvania, West Virginia, Ohio, Indiana, and Illinois throughout the first half of the nineteenth century.

Northwest Territory—Territory established by Congress during the 1780s. It would include the future states of Ohio, Indiana, Illinois, Wisconsin, and Michigan.

Oregon Country—Region of the American West that included the modern-day states of Washington, Oregon, and Idaho.

prairie schooner—Smaller, lighter covered wagon used primarily on western wagon trains following the California and Oregon Trails.

roustabout—Unskilled railroad worker who engaged in physical labor.

section—Refers to a portion of a township. The measurement was used in the United States beginning in the 1780s. A section measures one mile square and includes 640 acres.

shop locomotive—Special construction train that carries tools and equipment used to lay railroad tracks.

township—A land system established by Congress during the 1780s. A township measured six miles by six miles square and was divided into sections, each one mile square.

Trans-Appalachian West—Region of the United States that was frontier land between 1750 and the early 1800s. It generally includes the lands just west of the Appalachian Mountains.

Transcontinental Railroad—Railroad line constructed between 1864 and 1869 that stretched across the continental United States and connected to existing lines both to the east and west.

Trans-Mississippi Frontier—Frontier lands lying west of the Mississippi River.

The West—Once referred to the American frontier. Today, it usually refers to the region of the United States west of the Rocky Mountains.

Barter, James. *A Worker on the Transcontinental Railroad*. San Diego, Calif.: Lucent Books, 2003.

Dolan, Edward F. *The Transcontinental Railroad*. New York: Benchmark Books, 2003.

Evans, Clark J. *The Central Pacific Railroad*. New York: Children's Press, 2003.

Halpern, Monica. *Railroad Fever: Building the Transcontinental Railroad 1830–1870*. New York: National Geographic Children's Books, 2004.

Houghton, Gillian. *The Transcontinental Railroad: A Primary Source History of America's First Coast-to-Coast Railroad*. New York: Rosen Central Primary Source, 2003.

Meltzer, Milton. *Hear That Train Whistle Blow!: How the Railroad Changed the World*. New York: Random House, 2004.

Perl, Lila. *The Golden Mountain: The Story of the Chinese Who Built the Transcontinental Railroad*. New York: Benchmark Books, 2003.

Thompson, Linda. *The Transcontinental Railroad*. Vero Beach, Fla.: Rourke Publishing, 2005.

Uschan, Michael V. *The Transcontinental Railroad*. Milwaukee, Wis.: World Almanac Library, 2004.

Central Pacific Railroad Photographic History Museum
<http://cprr.org>

Transcontinental Railroad, PBS.Org
<http://www.pbs.org/>

In the "Search" box, type "Transcontinental Railroad American Experience" and click the "Go" button. Click on the "American Experience Transcontinental Railroad" link.

Union Pacific: History and Photos
<http://www.up.com>

Put cursor over "General Public." When new text appears below, move cursor down and then left, and click on "History & Photos."

California State Railroad Museum
111 "I" Street
Sacramento, CA 95814
(916) 445-6645

Golden Spike National Historic Site
P.O. Box 897
Brigham City, UT 84302-0897
(435) 471-2209

The Union Pacific Railroad Museum
200 Pearl Street
Council Bluffs, IA 51503
(712) 329-8307